D0812685

# The Vietnam War

**Other books in the History Firsthand series:**

# The Vietnam War

Tamara L. Roleff, *Book Editor*

Daniel Leone, *President*
Bonnie Szumski, *Publisher*
Scott Barbour, *Managing Editor*
David M. Haugen, *Series Editor*

Greenhaven Press, Inc., San Diego, California

Every effort has been made to trace the owners of copyrighted material. The articles in this volume may have been edited for content, length, and/or reading level. The titles have been changed to enhance the editorial purpose.

No part of this book may be reproduced or used in any form or by any means, electrical, mechanical, or otherwise, including, but not limited to, photocopy, recording, or any information storage and retrieval system, without prior permission from the publisher.

Library of Congress Cataloging-in-Publication Data

The Vietnam War / Tamara L. Roleff, book editor.
    p.  cm. — (History firsthand)
    Includes bibliographical references and index.
    ISBN 0-7377-0887-5 (lib. bdg. : alk. paper) —
    ISBN 0-7377-0886-7 (pbk. : alk. paper)
    1. Vietnamese Conflict, 1961–1975—United States. I. Roleff,
Tamara L., 1959– II. Series.

DS558 .V46   2002
959.704'3373—dc21                 2001028924

Cover photo: © Bettmann/CORBIS
National Archives, 78, 84, 134, 140

Copyright © 2002 by Greenhaven Press, Inc.
10911 Technology Place, San Diego, CA 92127

Printed in the USA

# Contents

## Chapter 1: The War at Home

**1. Thoughts About Induction**     37
*by Tim O'Brien*
A college graduate faces the draft and the prospect of
going to war. He considers his options of evading the
draft or protesting the war, but the shame and disgrace such actions would bring on him and his family
compel him to report as scheduled.

**2. Draft Dodger**     44
*by Ron Stone*
A college student's local draft board determines he
has had enough time to graduate and orders him to report for induction into the Army. Vowing never to
fight in a war he does not believe in, he flees to
Canada.

**3. Conscientious Objector**     54
*by David Brown*
The Army is sometimes unwilling to grant conscientious objector status to its soldiers. In one case, it denied a soldier's CO application, and when he refused
to obey orders during basic training, he was jailed,
court-martialed, dishonorably discharged, and then
imprisoned in a federal penitentiary.

**4. Vietnam Veterans Against the War**     65
*by John F. Kerry*
Thousands of veterans of the war were horrified by
what they had seen and done in Vietnam. When they
returned to the United States, they organized the Vietnam Veterans Against the War organization to protest
the senseless and needless deaths in Vietnam. One
member speaks in front of Congress, urging it to end
the war.

# Chapter 2: Combat

# Chapter 3: In the Rear

interruptions, choose what he wanted to eat, explore a beautiful city, and forget about the war.

# Chapter 4: Wounded in Action

to help out during a busy period, and she felt over-whelmed by the injuries and death she faced.

# Chapter 5: Prisoner of War

# Chapter 6: The Enemy

# Foreword

In his preface to a book on the events leading to the Civil War, Stephen B. Oates, the historian and biographer of Abraham Lincoln, John Brown, and other noteworthy American historical figures, explained the difficulty of writing history in the traditional third-person voice of the biographer and historian. "The trouble, I realized, was the detached third-person voice," wrote Oates. "It seemed to wring all the life out of my characters and the antebellum era." Indeed, how can a historian, even one as prominent as Oates, compete with the eloquent voices of Daniel Webster, Abraham Lincoln, Harriet Beecher Stowe, Frederick Douglass, and Robert E. Lee?

Oates's comment notwithstanding, every student of history, professional and amateur alike, can name a score of excellent accounts written in the traditional third-person voice of the historian that bring to life an event or an era and the people who lived through it. In *Battle Cry of Freedom*, James M. McPherson vividly re-creates the American Civil War. Barbara Tuchman's *The Guns of August* captures in sharp detail the tensions in Europe that led to the outbreak of World War I. Taylor Branch's *Parting the Waters* provides a detailed and dramatic account of the American Civil Rights Movement. The study of history would be impossible without such guiding texts.

Nonetheless, Oates's comment makes a compelling point. Often the most convincing tellers of history are those who lived through the event, the eyewitnesses who recorded their firsthand experiences in autobiographies, speeches, memoirs, journals, and letters. The Greenhaven Press History Firsthand series presents history through the words of first-person narrators. Each text in this series captures a significant historical era or event—the American Civil War, the

Great Depression, the Holocaust, the Roaring Twenties, the 1960s, the Vietnam War. Readers will investigate these historical eras and events by examining primary-source documents, authored by chroniclers both famous and little known. The texts in the History Firsthand series comprise the celebrated and familiar words of the presidents, generals, and famous men and women of letters who recorded their impressions for posterity, as well as the statements of the ordinary people who struggled to understand the storm of events around them—the foot soldiers who fought the great battles and their loved ones back home, the men and women who waited on the breadlines, the college students who marched in protest.

The texts in this series are particularly suited to students beginning serious historical study. By examining these firsthand documents, novice historians can begin to form their own insights and conclusions about the historical era or event under investigation. To aid the student in that process, the texts in the History Firsthand series include introductions that provide an overview of the era or event, timelines, and bibliographies that point the serious student toward key historical works for further study.

The study of history commences with an examination of words—the testimony of witnesses who lived through an era or event and left for future generations the task of making sense of their accounts. The Greenhaven Press History Firsthand series invites the beginner historian to commence the process of historical investigation by focusing on the words of those individuals who made history by living through it and recording their experiences firsthand.

# Introduction: A History of the Vietnam War

The history of the Vietnam War begins long before the United States became embroiled in the conflict during the 1960s. The roots of the war go back more than two thousand years, when the Chinese conquered and ruled parts of Vietnam. The Vietnamese were continually at war (militarily as well as culturally) with China in an attempt to preserve their national identity. Then in the 1800s the French colonized Vietnam. Vietnamese partisans appeared and organized a nationalist movement, but France maintained its rule. In 1940, Japan swept into Vietnam, crushing the French, and the Vietnamese had another enemy in their battle for independence.

In 1941, Ho Chi Minh (meaning "He Who Enlightens"), a Vietnamese nationalist who had studied in France and Russia, organized a group to resist the Japanese. He formed the Communist-inspired Vietnam Independence League—*Viet Nam Doc Lap Dong Minh*—whose followers became known as the Viet Minh. Ho Chi Minh worked with the United States during World War II to defeat the Japanese in Southeast Asia, hoping that when the war was over, America would support Vietnam's independence. In 1945, following Japan's defeat, Ho proclaimed his country's independence as the Democratic Republic of Vietnam. Borrowing phrases from America's Declaration of Independence, Ho told his audience,

> We hold the truth that all men are created equal, that they are endowed by their Creator with certain unalienable rights, among them life, liberty and the pursuit of happiness.[1]

Bao Dai, the puppet emperor under the French and the Japanese, abdicated to Ho and the Viet Minh. Much to Ho's disappointment, however, most of the world would not recognize the new democratic republic and the French refused to leave Vietnam. A compromise agreement between Ho and the French gave the northern part of Vietnam to the Viet Minh and the south to the French. Elections would be held in the south to decide who should govern the divided nation. Sensing that the South Vietnamese would vote for the Viet Minh, France later canceled the elections and demanded that the Viet Minh surrender all power in the north. Ho's response was to attack the French, setting off a war.

Ho still hoped that the United States would support Vietnam's independence movement, but although President Harry S. Truman supported an independent Vietnam, he would not support a Communist Vietnam. France offered another compromise as a solution to the war. The compromise gave Vietnam its semi-independence in the form of an associated statehood (instead of its colonial status) and reinstalled Bao Dai as its puppet leader. For the United States, an associated statehood was a good start toward independence, and on February 7, 1950, it recognized the State of Vietnam. Ho and the Viet Minh, however, refused to accept the validity of an associate statehood. They yearned for a united Vietnam, free of outside interests.

In the ensuing years, American politicians became almost fanatical about defeating the "Red Menace," a term they coined for communism, both at home and abroad. Dean Rusk, America's undersecretary of state, gave a hint of what was to come when he announced that "the resources of the United States would be deployed to reserve Indochina and Southeast Asia from further Communist encroachment."[2] The French openly used this policy for their own gain; by 1954, the United States was financing nearly 80 percent of France's expenses in its war with Vietnam. Meanwhile, the Viet Minh were receiving military aid from Communist China, much to the alarm of the United States.

## Fighting the French

Ho and his commanding general, Vo Nguyen Giap, developed a three-step strategy to win the war with France. First, they would use guerrilla tactics, ambushing French troops and then fleeing into the jungle to minimize their own casualties. Then, they would graduate to attacking the French at their weakest points, and finally, they would fight in full-fledged battles. Ho recruited villagers and peasants, including women and children, who would aid the Viet Minh by offering food, shelter, and their own bodies in the war against the French. He wanted to erode French support for the war by dragging the war out, hoping that eventually the French would lose patience with it and leave Vietnam to the Vietnamese.

Through years of hit-and-run attacks, skirmishes, and battles, Ho and Giap gradually wore down the French resolve to stay in Vietnam. The final straw was the decisive Viet Minh victory at Dien Bien Phu in 1954. The French believed their camp in this fortified city near the Laotian border was an "impregnable fortress."[3] Giap would soon prove them wrong. Giap had 37,500 frontline combat troops and another 10,000 in reserve to fight the French. He also had the support of approximately 300,000 peasants committed to keeping the supply and communication lines open from China, about five hundred miles to the north. On March 13, 1954, Giap began the siege of Dien Bien Phu, which did not end until the French surrendered on May 7. That same day, a delegation of nine nations met in Geneva to discuss the fate of Vietnam.

In July, a cease-fire agreement was signed by Vietnam and France. The agreement, known as the Geneva Accords, split Vietnam into two sections at the seventeenth parallel of latitude with a six-mile-wide demilitarized zone (DMZ). The Viet Minh, led by Ho Chi Minh, were allowed to govern the Democratic Republic of Vietnam north of the seventeenth parallel, while the French troops were moved to the southern half of Vietnam. Ngo Dinh Diem, an anti-Communist, was named president of the Republic of Vietnam (South Vietnam). The Geneva Accords called for elections to be held in the south in two years, but everyone involved knew that if elections were held, South Vietnam would vote Communist.

The United States was determined that Vietnam would not become Communist. President Dwight D. Eisenhower, and American presidents following him, strongly believed in the "domino theory" of communism; if South Vietnam became Communist, then all its neighboring Asian countries would soon fall to communism, much as one standing domino topples the next. To prevent the fall of South Vietnam, the United States began providing financial and military aid to Diem to keep his government in place. Though pro-American, Diem was an ineffective and unpopular leader. The Vietnamese people began to hate Diem and the United States as much as they had hated France.

As expected, the 1956 elections were canceled. Meanwhile, the Viet Minh (who changed their name to Viet Cong in 1960) continued recruiting and organizing peasants and villagers in the south. They were being trained to fight the Army of the Republic of Victnam (ARVN), which Diem depended on to retain his power.

## U.S. Policy in Vietnam

The situation in Southeast Asia worsened during the 1960s. The Soviet Union was involving itself in a civil war in Laos. The Viet Cong (VC) were getting more active, using the Ho Chi Minh Trail (a supply trail that started in North Vietnam and wound its way through Laos and Cambodia) to deliver supplies to secret VC strongholds in South Vietnam in preparation for a coming conflict. President John F. Kennedy warned the world in his inaugural address in 1961 that the United States was absolutely opposed to communism. America, he proclaimed, "shall pay any price, bear any burden, meet any hardship, support any friend, oppose any foe, to assure the survival and the success of liberty."[4] To support his promises, the United States started sending military advisers to South Vietnam. In 1961, about nine hundred advisers were in South Vietnam teaching the South Vietnamese army everything from how to use American weapons to how to play baseball. A year later, the number of advisers had risen to eleven thousand.

As part of the strategy to defeat the Viet Cong, the South Vietnamese government, with the help of American advisers, destroyed South Vietnamese villages, forcefully moving the peasants into fortified stockades called "strategic hamlets." The idea behind this drastic and ill-fated measure was to isolate South Vietnam citizens and prevent them from helping or joining the Viet Cong. In reality, it only caused the villagers to resent the ARVN forces and the United States for moving them from homes and lands that had been in their families for generations. Many villagers subsequently became secret supporters of the Viet Cong as a result of this disastrous initiative.

In 1962, U.S. advisers began to accompany South Vietnamese soldiers during their assaults against suspected VC strongholds. As more and more American weapons, supplies, and troops poured into Vietnam in the early 1960s, South Vietnamese soldiers became increasingly reluctant to fight the Viet Cong themselves. They were more than willing to let U.S. advisers fight their battles for them. Yet despite the fact that several Americans had been killed in action, Kennedy denied in a 1962 news conference that U.S. troops were fighting in Vietnam. This example of dishonesty by an American leader concerning policy in Vietnam was a trend that would continue for many years under several presidents.

By 1963, the Viet Cong were so strong that twenty-three thousand U.S. advisers were in Vietnam and more were preparing to deploy. The situation was such that Kennedy had to decide whether to increase American support dramatically—something he was not anxious to do with an election approaching—or withdraw from Vietnam and face the prospect of South Vietnam falling to the Communists. Kennedy realized that no matter how many advisers and how much materiel the United States sent to Vietnam, the only way the war against the Viet Cong could be won was if the South Vietnamese themselves supported the war. He told news anchor Walter Cronkite in October 1963 that the

South Vietnamese

> are the ones who have to win it or lose it. We can help them, we
> can give them equipment, we can send our men out there as ad-
> visers, but they have to win it, the people of Vietnam, against the
> Communists. We are prepared to assist them, but I don't think that
> the war can be won unless the people support the effort and, in my
> opinion, in the last two months, the government has gotten out of
> touch with the people.[5]

In fact, Diem had been out of touch with the people of
South Vietnam for more than the past few months. He and
the rest of his family were almost universally despised by
American advisers, South Vietnamese generals, Buddhist
religious leaders, and most of the South Vietnamese. With
American knowledge and support, Diem's generals staged
a coup against him on November 1, 1963. He and his wife
Nhu were assassinated the next day. Three weeks later,
Kennedy himself was assassinated.

# War Starts Between the United States and Vietnam

Lyndon B. Johnson, who succeeded Kennedy as president
after he was shot, also hoped to delay a decision about committing more American troops to Vietnam until after the
presidential election in 1964. In fact, he campaigned that
"we are not about to send American boys nine or ten thousand miles away from home to do what Asian boys ought to
be doing for themselves."[6] However, an attack by North
Vietnamese patrol boats on two U.S. destroyers in the Gulf
of Tonkin in August 1964—an incident that some critics
claim was provoked by the United States because the ships
were inside North Vietnam's territorial waters—forced him
to act otherwise. Johnson ordered retaliatory air strikes
against North Vietnam. It was during these air raids that
North Vietnam captured its first American prisoner of war,
Everett Alvarez Jr. A few days later, Congress passed the
Gulf of Tonkin Resolution, which gave the president autho-
rization "to take all necessary measures to repel any armed

attack against the forces of the United States and to prevent further aggression."[7]

Although Johnson had made campaign promises not to escalate U.S. involvement in the war in Vietnam, he decided after the election that the United States must send troops to help South Vietnam defeat the Viet Cong partisans and the newly forming regular units of the North Vietnamese Army (NVA). The South Vietnamese government was extremely unstable; after the coup and assassination of Diem, seven leaders had come and gone in 1964 alone. Johnson himself was so fed up with the successive coups that he decided that only strong American intervention in Vietnam would prevent the Communists from taking over. Johnson's top advisers visited South Vietnam in 1964 and 1965 and informed him that the war was lost unless the United States stepped in with combat troops. They believed that South Vietnam would start to take responsibility for its survival only if the United States showed that it, too, was willing "to take serious risks"[8] in the fight against communism. Other advisers, however, warned that the South Vietnamese Army would have no incentive to fight the Viet Cong if American soldiers were there to do the job for them.

A few attacks by Viet Cong troops on American and ARVN forces outraged Johnson. In November and December 1964, Viet Cong troops attacked two U.S. bases; ambushed two companies of South Vietnamese rangers, killing nearly two hundred soldiers; and planted a car bomb at a Saigon hotel that housed American officers. In total, fifteen Americans and more than two hundred South Vietnamese were killed; hundreds more were wounded.

Johnson ordered extensive retaliatory bombing raids against the north from February through April 1965, in operations code-named Flaming Dart and Rolling Thunder (which continued through November 1968). U.S. bombers flew thirty-six hundred missions just in April, bombing bridges, power plants, fuel depots, factories, and army camps in the north. However, the eight weeks of bombing had no effect on North Vietnam's military or economic capability, according to American military reports, since North Vietnam received most of its military supplies from China and the Soviet Union. Realizing that the bombing was not as effective against the Viet Cong as he had hoped, Johnson finally acceded to his generals' demands to send in combat troops. In March 1965, two battalions of U.S. Marines landed at Da Nang to provide protection for the American airfield there. These soldiers would only be the first of many. By the end of the year, nearly 200,000 American troops would be in Vietnam.

## A Limited War

When Johnson authorized the deployment of combat troops to Vietnam, he and his advisers decided to impose certain conditions on the war. The war would be a "limited" war. According to General Earle G. Wheeler, chairman of the Joint Chiefs of Staff, America's goal in Vietnam was not the total defeat of the North Vietnamese Army and Viet Cong, but "to get the nations in that part of the world to leave their neighbors alone, free to find their own destiny without out-side pressure."[9] In addition, Johnson decreed that the war would be fought within the boundaries of Vietnam. American troops would not be permitted to fight in the neighboring countries of Laos or Cambodia. He also would not authorize the invasion or "liberation" of North Vietnam by U.S. troops. Johnson feared that any of these actions would antagonize the Soviet Union or China (both of which were already giving North Vietnam aid and supplies) into joining the war against the United States and possibly lead to another world war.

Johnson and his advisers planned, at least initially, to fight a war of attrition. U.S. forces would be used to destroy Communist soldiers, supplies, and war-related targets. Their plan was to keep North Vietnam so busy rebuilding that it would not be able to continue fighting the war. This would give South Vietnam the time it so desperately needed to recover and rebuild its own forces so that it could fight without help from American soldiers.

Although Johnson's limitations on the war were well intended, it was a disastrous military policy. Prohibiting U.S. troops from fighting in Laos or Cambodia prevented them from destroying the Ho Chi Minh Trail that the NVA and the VC used to resupply their forces in the south. The limits also allowed the enemy to establish base camps across the border from South Vietnam where they were safe from pursuing U.S. troops. These conditions on U.S. involvement in the war fit in perfectly with Ho and Giap's plans. Like the war with the French, the war with the Americans would be a war of wills. They hoped that America, like France, would eventually tire of the war and leave Vietnam.

## Fighting the War

The United States could not envision ever leaving Vietnam without having accomplished its goals. American combat troops had access to—and made good use of—high-tech equipment such as helicopters, fighter planes, bombers, and ships that could bomb targets many miles inland. The use of helicopters in medical evacuations (medevacs) was perfected during the Vietnam War and saved thousands of lives by getting the injured to hospitals within minutes of being wounded. Helicopters also ferried men and supplies to remote jungle posts and could provide instant support for troops in battle. Vietnam also saw the use of new warfighting tools such as napalm, a gasoline-based gel used to burn down the jungle where the NVA and VC were hiding, and Agent Orange, a defoliant also used to deny jungle cover to the enemy.

Used to fighting traditional battles in which the opposing forces lined up and shot at each other, the United States was at a distinct disadvantage in Vietnam. The Viet Cong specialized in guerrilla tactics; their hit-and-run attacks, ambushes, and booby traps frustrated U.S. troops. Unable to find and kill enemy soldiers, American soldiers sometimes vented their fear and anger on Vietnamese civilians. Since the war was essentially a civil war between Communist-led forces in the north and the anti-Communist forces in the south, it was extremely difficult—if not impossible—for Americans to know who the enemy was. Many Vietnamese were double agents, working for the Americans or South Vietnamese during the day and aiding the VC at night. E.J. Banks, a Marine captain in Vietnam, explains why many Americans were hostile to all the Vietnamese they met:

> You never knew who was the enemy and who was the friend. They all looked alike. They all dressed alike. They were all Vietnamese. Some of them were Vietcong. Here's a woman of twenty-two or twenty-three. She is pregnant, and she tells an interrogator that her husband works in Danang and isn't a Vietcong. But she watches your men walk down a trail and get killed or wounded by a booby trap. She knows the booby trap is there, but she doesn't warn them. Maybe she planted it herself. . . . The enemy was all around you.[10]

Contributing to the Americans' confusion was that they could seldom declare a complete victory. They could never completely "secure" or clear a village or an area of the enemy. As soon as U.S. troops left, the VC came back. Many troops became demoralized when they had to return to the same areas over and over again in a futile attempt to drive the enemy out. Although a few combat units were skilled at guerrilla warfare, the Viet Cong generally won these battles against the Americans. The U.S. troops won the more traditional battles, such as in the Ia Drang valley in 1965 and the battles of Khe Sanh and Hue, that were proof of the major NVA assault against the south in 1968.

## The Tet Offensive

General Giap started his big offensive on January 21, 1968, against the Americans at Khe Sanh, a Marine base just south of the DMZ near the Laotian border. Giap chose to attack right before Tet, a major Vietnamese holiday. In the past, both sides had traditionally observed a cease-fire during the festival, and Giap knew that half the South Vietnamese soldiers and many American troops would be on leave from their duties. Khe Sanh was not the main objective during the offensive, however; the purpose of the assault by thirty-five thousand North Vietnamese soldiers was to distract the Americans from the buildup of NVA and VC forces that were preparing to attack other major cities and towns throughout South Vietnam. Ho and Giap were planning a grand revolt against the south called "General Offensive, General Uprising." The theory was that the South Vietnamese people would join in the uprising against the hated Americans and the Saigon government. Khe Sanh was just the beginning of the plan that was to end with a great military victory for the north.

At first it appeared that Ho and Giap would succeed. For ten days, Americans were riveted to their television sets as news reporters told of the siege of Khe Sanh. Then, on January 31, 1968, Americans and South Vietnamese were stunned by the coordinated NVA and VC attacks on more than one hundred of South Vietnam's largest cities and towns, including Saigon and Hue, and more than twenty American military bases. They were equally shocked to see the American embassy in Saigon under attack. It took nearly seven hours of fierce fighting and five American casualties before the squad of nineteen VC soldiers who attacked the embassy were killed or captured. Some battles, such as the battle at the embassy, were quickly fought. In others, however, it took days or even weeks before U.S. and ARVN troops could drive the enemy out of the cities. The Americans and South Vietnamese faced bloody hand-to-hand and house-to-house fighting in the city of Hue before it was finally liberated on February 23.

When the smoke cleared from all the battles across South Vietnam, Giap had suffered a major defeat. It would take the NVA and VC years to recover from their losses during the Tet Offensive. Of the 84,000 Viet Cong troops who participated in the battles throughout the south, between 37,000 and 45,000 were killed. American casualties were comparatively light: 2,600 dead and nearly 13,000 wounded. Despite the north's devastating losses, most Americans believed that the United States had lost the battle, and, in effect, the war, a view that was promulgated by the media.

## The Media and the War

Americans were extremely confused by the Tet Offensive. Their president and his military leaders had been telling them for years that the United States was winning the war and that it would soon be over. In fact, just a few months before the Tet Offensive, General William C. Westmoreland, commander of the American forces in Vietnam, had told Congress that the war would be over in about two more years. So Americans were shocked by such a strong show of force by an enemy that was supposedly almost defeated. Westmoreland tried to explain that "historically a force on the downgrade often tries to recover by means of some spectacular surge."[11] The media's coverage of the Tet Offensive infuriated him; he fumed that the press and television transformed "what was undeniably a catastrophic military defeat for the enemy into a presumed debacle for Americans and South Vietnamese."[12] His complaint was accurate; few reporters explained to their readers or viewers that the Tet Offensive was actually a significant victory for the United States and South Vietnam.

The Tet Offensive had an immense psychological impact on Americans and was the turning point in the war in the States. It was an example of the "credibility gap" that had existed since 1965 between what the Johnson Administration was telling Americans about the war and what the media was reporting. When Johnson told them U.S. forces would soon be coming home, he was secretly increasing the number of troops he was sending to Vietnam. On March 10, 1968, the *New York Times* printed a front-page story about Westmoreland requesting another 200,000 troops. Americans wondered why additional troops were needed if the U.S. and ARVN forces had won such a victory against the Viet Cong. After the Tet Offensive, public opinion polls showed that 49 percent of Americans thought the war was "a mistake."

# War Protests

The American public's perception of the Tet Offensive and its accompanying credibility gap was a big boost for the antiwar movement. Americans had been protesting the war for many years, but in 1968 the clash between "doves" and "hawks" nearly tore the country apart.

War protesters, sometimes called "doves," were against the war for many reasons. Some did not believe that a Communist Vietnam threatened the interests or national security of the United States. They argued that the war was a civil war between North and South Vietnam and that the United States had no business supporting either side. "Doves" also maintained that Americans and American technology were killing tens of thousands of innocent Vietnamese, a practice that had to stop. Many protesters were students, but people from almost every segment of society, including veterans of the war, housewives, civil rights leaders, ministers, and members of the news and entertainment industry, were also against the war.

Many Americans, however, were aghast that others were protesting the war. These people, called "hawks," believed in and trusted their government. If the government said it was necessary to fight in Vietnam to prevent the spread of communism, then they supported the war. They were incensed with the protesters for doubting their government's policies and decisions and for refusing to do their duty by serving in the military.

Adding fuel to the protests over the morality of the Vietnam War was the news in 1969 that U.S. lieutenant William L. Calley Jr. and his platoon killed several hundred Vietnamese peasants in a village called My Lai on March 16, 1968. Not only were the villagers murdered, they were also raped, sodomized, tortured, and mutilated. Calley and twelve other officers and enlisted men were charged with war crimes, but only Calley was convicted of the charge of murdering twenty-two unarmed civilians. The others were acquitted or the charges against them were dropped. In 1971, Calley was sentenced to life imprisonment, later reduced to ten years, and paroled in 1974. Many wondered how such an atrocity could be committed if American aims were so noble.

## America Begins to Get Out of Vietnam

Beset by the public's perception that the war was lost after the Tet Offensive, poll results showing declining support for the war, and the widening credibility gap, Johnson announced in a nationally televised speech that he was halting the bombing over North Vietnam. In addition, he was sending a representative to North Vietnam to try to negotiate a peace settlement to end the war. Finally, he pledged to work for peace in Vietnam for the rest of the year. Then he dropped his bombshell, almost as an afterthought. "I shall not seek, and I will not accept, the nomination of my party for another term as your President,"[13] he told an astonished audience. Almost no one was aware of his plan to step aside as president. His health was beginning to decline, and he was willing to let another president try to end the war.

Although peace talks started in Paris in May, little was accomplished. The Americans insisted that the North Vietnamese withdraw from South Vietnam, while the Communists demanded that the South Vietnamese government include Viet Cong representatives. Both sides refused to consider the other's demands, and the peace talks continued off and on for five years before a resolution was finally achieved.

Meanwhile, Richard M. Nixon was elected president, partly because he said he had a secret plan to end the war in Vietnam. After the election, he slowly revealed his program to have "peace with honor" in Vietnam. Nixon's policy of "Vietnamization" was a three-part strategy, one part of which he kept secret from the public for several years. Americans were told that he would withdraw U.S. troops from Vietnam (which had peaked at 543,400 in June 1969) and transfer the responsibility of fighting the Viet Cong over to the South Vietnamese army. The United States would give the ARVN military equipment, such as rifles, machine guns, grenade launchers, mortars, planes, boats, helicopters, and trucks, and advisers to teach them how to use them, but the South Vietnamese would have to fight without U.S. troops.

Nixon also worked to improve relations with China and the Soviet Union. He opened talks with the Soviets on arms control, hoping that the Russians might be able to influence the North Vietnamese to accept a peace treaty. He also relaxed a trade embargo against China with the same hope. He learned during his talks with these two countries that they would not object militarily if the United States was to expand the war into Laos and Cambodia as long as it did not invade North Vietnam or try to overthrow its government. This was an important concession, because Nixon's third, and secret, strategy was to authorize the secret bombing of the Ho Chi Minh Trail and other Communist strongholds in Laos and Cambodia.

The *New York Times* leaked the story of the proposed secret bombings in Cambodia in May 1969, but the public showed little interest. Nixon believed that as long as no ground troops were involved and there were few American casualties, he would receive little opposition from the public. His theory was to prove accurate. On April 30, 1970, a force of twenty thousand U.S. and ARVN troops attacked two main NVA and VC outposts in Cambodia, although the enemy forces had fled the area a few weeks earlier in anticipation of the raids. Nixon announced the invasion on television that night and asked the nation to support his decision:

> If when the chips are down, the world's most powerful nation acts like a pitiful, helpless giant, the forces of totalitarianism and anarchy will threaten free nations and free institutions throughout the world.[14]

Many Americans had no intention of supporting Nixon's decision. They were infuriated by the invasion. Not only was the invasion illegal and immoral, but it was an expansion of the war that Nixon had promised to end. Riots and protests erupted all over the country, especially on college campuses. Kent State University in Ohio was the scene of a particularly violent riot that the police were not able to contain. The governor then called in the National Guard. When student protesters refused to disperse, the Guard opened fire. Four students were killed and nine more were wounded. America erupted into more protests against the senseless deaths; seventy-five thousand protesters marched on Washington, D.C., a few days later.

Congress was also angry about of the secret invasion of Cambodia. In retaliation, it repealed the Gulf of Tonkin Resolution, which in 1964 had given the president the authority to use armed force in Southeast Asia. Senator J. William Fulbright believed that Nixon's Vietnamization policies were "undermining the security of our country" and that "it might be a long time before the sun shines again"[15] in the United States. He led the Senate in passing a resolution prohibiting U.S. forces from fighting in Cambodia, although it failed to pass in the House.

## The Pentagon Papers

A major blow to American and foreign support of the Vietnam War came in June 1971 when the *New York Times* started publishing excerpts of a secret government study on U.S. involvement in the war. Daniel Ellsberg, a former Defense Department employee, had leaked the secret report to the newspaper. Known as the Pentagon Papers, the documents revealed how each presidential administration, beginning with Truman and continuing on through Eisenhower, Kennedy, and Johnson, had lied to the American public and Congress about its intentions, ignored international laws and treaties, and manipulated the government in Saigon for its own ends. The publication of the Pentagon Papers convinced many Americans that the war was wrong and that their government knew it. Nixon ordered the Justice Department to seek an injunction to prevent the *New York Times* and other newspapers from printing any more excerpts of the study. The newspapers appealed the injunction all the way to the Supreme Court, which ruled in favor of the *New York Times*.

The publication of the Pentagon Papers was ultimately the cause of Nixon's downfall a few years later. The White House ordered a break-in of the office of Ellsberg's psychiatrist in an attempt to find some incriminating or disparaging information about him. This burglary and its subsequent cover-up would come to light during the Watergate scandal that would force Nixon to resign in 1974.

## The Spring Offensive

In the meantime, Nixon sent his national security adviser Henry Kissinger to meet in secret with North Vietnamese negotiator Le Duc Tho, without a representative from South Vietnam present. The two men met for two years without reaching an agreement, and the situation appeared to worsen when the North Vietnamese launched an attack on March 30, 1972, known as the Spring Offensive. The North Vietnamese sent 120,000 troops across the border into South Vietnam in three waves—in the northern provinces, along the central highlands, and into the Mekong delta near Saigon. Only 70,000 U.S. troops remained in South Vietnam, of which only 6,000 were combat troops. The South Vietnamese army had more than 1 million soldiers, yet it still took them nearly six months to push the North Vietnamese back. They would have failed utterly if the United States had not supplied advisers to take command of the disorganized ARVN forces and B-52 bombers to fly 5,000 missions during the attacks. The United States also mined the northern harbor at Haiphong, despite fears that it would derail plans for a peace summit with the Soviet Union that spring.

## Peace Talks

The bombing of North Vietnam took its toll, and the Viet Cong were more willing to talk peace in the fall of 1972. Both sides appeared willing to make compromises they had been unwilling to make earlier. The United States was willing to permit the NVA to keep some of its troops in the south, and American forces would be withdrawn within sixty days. North Vietnam no longer insisted that South Vietnam's President Nguyen Van Thieu abdicate to the NVA, and it would return American prisoners of war. A council made up of North and South Vietnamese would be formed to supervise national elections and determine the fate of South Vietnam. Everything appeared set for the cease-fire and treaty until South Vietnam's President Thieu rejected the agreement. He knew that, with this agreement, he had no chance to stay in power once the Americans left Vietnam.

With the negotiations falling apart, Le Duc Tho disclosed in an October 1972 broadcast that a settlement had been reached in secret meetings. Kissinger was forced to hold a news conference to declare, "We believe that peace is at hand. We believe that an agreement is within sight."[16] Nixon, however, believed that Kissinger's statements unrealistically raised Americans' expectations for peace, and so publicly repudiated him, stating that there were still differences that needed to be resolved.

By this time, Nixon had been reelected in a landslide in November. The North Vietnamese had been hoping to have an agreement in place before the election, but they were still negotiating the terms then. The peace talks between Tho and Kissinger broke down again in December. Nixon gave the North Vietnamese an ultimatum, and when they did not respond, he ordered massive bombing raids over North Vietnam. Starting December 18, and continuing every day except Christmas through December 29, American B-52 bombers flew nearly 3,000 missions, dropping bombs on Hanoi and Haiphong. Many Americans were furious with Nixon, believing that he was escalating the war again when peace seemed so close at hand. Nixon intended the bombing to be a show of force to the North Vietnamese, and to Thieu, to show that the United States would come to the south's aid if the north broke the agreement.

The peace talks resumed in January 1973. The agreement reached had a few changed words, but the basic content remained. Despite Thieu's objections, it was signed on January 27, 1973. "We have finally achieved peace with honor,"[17] Nixon told America. Among the provisions already agreed to in the October treaty, North and South Vietnam agreed to a complicated cease-fire; U.S. bases in Vietnam were to be dismantled; and American forces were to leave Vietnam within sixty days of the return of American POWs. The final remaining 27,000 American troops in South Vietnam, along with the last of the 591 prisoners of war held by the North Vietnamese, left on March 29, 1973.

## The Fall of South Vietnam

The war between North and South Vietnam did not end when the United States pulled out in March 1973. In fact, it was not long before North and South Vietnam were fighting again. President Thieu had little hope of defeating the north without help. He was not a popular leader, and he was forced to use the south's military troops to keep him in power instead of using them to fight the Communists. Thieu expected that the United States would help him continue the war against North Vietnam, but Americans were tired of war. Once all the troops were home, most did not care about what happened in Southeast Asia. Congress passed the War Powers Act in November 1973, which prohibited the president from committing U.S. troops without congressional approval. In addition, Congress passed another law that prevented U.S. troops from being deployed to a war zone for more than ninety days without congressional approval. So, despite the provisions made in the treaty, South Vietnam was, for the first time, solely responsible for its own self-defense.

Now that the U.S. involvement in Vietnam was over, Nixon was too absorbed in his own problems at home to worry about South Vietnam anymore. The burglary of the Democratic National Convention Headquarters at the Watergate Hotel in Washington, D.C., was the focus of attention for both Nixon and the country. Since the president was implicated in the scandal, Nixon resigned on August 9, 1974, and was replaced by Vice President Gerald R. Ford.

At the same time, North Vietnam began another offensive against the south. It had a two-year plan to conquer South Vietnam, but in actuality, it took only eight months. The north began with continuous attacks against cities in the south. Thieu and the south's generals decided to concentrate their forces in the southern half of the country, so they ceded the northern provinces to the NVA. When the generals and their armies began their retreat before the NVA, the rest of the south panicked, and provinces quickly fell before the advancing northern army. In April 1975, the NVA was ready to enter Saigon. Thieu abdicated to General Duong Van Minh and fled the capital.

There were still some Americans in Saigon, mostly diplomatic personnel, news media, and a few military troops whose duties were to protect the embassy. U.S. officials delayed giving the order to evacuate the capital as long as possible, knowing that a withdrawal would cause panic among the Vietnamese. Playing the song "White Christmas" on a local radio station would be the signal for Americans to go to the embassy for evacuation. Despite the secrecy of the plan, thousands of South Vietnamese stormed the embassy in hopes of being evacuated with the Americans. The U.S. Marines kept flying helicopters until nearly 1,000 Americans and approximately 6,000 South Vietnamese had been airlifted to navy carriers off the coast. Two thousand of those evacuees had been rescued from the roof of the American embassy in Saigon. The last Americans left Saigon on April 30, 1975. Not long after, Minh surrendered to the North Vietnamese. He told Bui Tin, a journalist and former NVA officer, that he had waited all morning to transfer power to the North Vietnamese. Tin replied, "There is no question of your transferring power. Your power has crumbled. You have nothing in your hands to surrender and so you cannot surrender what you do not possess."[18] And with these words, Vietnam became one country again.

## Legacy

The Vietnam War changed America. Americans once had trusted and believed in their government, but after the war, they were not as ready to believe whatever their politicians and military leaders told them. Although most Americans agreed that the United States was fighting the Vietnam War for just, noble, and unselfish reasons—to stop the spread of communism—midway through the war, most Americans viewed the war as a mistake.

To their dismay, Americans learned that they were not the almighty world power they believed themselves to be. As Johnson and Nixon repeatedly told their advisers, the United States had never lost a war before, and they did not want to be the first president to do so. Losing this war—despite the heroic, valiant, and outstanding efforts of the U.S. military—was a shock to most Americans. Many believed then—and believe now—that their country should not enter a war unless it is totally committed to winning it. More than twenty-five years after the end of the Vietnam War, Americans still debate whether they should involve themselves in another country's problems. They continually point out that they do not want a future conflict to turn into "another Vietnam," meaning an unwinnable war.

For several years, Americans did not honor the veterans who had served in Vietnam. Many Americans routinely shunned and insulted veterans when they returned from Vietnam. They unfairly blamed the veterans for their country's policies and held all veterans responsible for the few atrocities they heard about in the war, such as the My Lai massacre. Returning veterans—both those who had volunteered and those who had been unwillingly drafted—were bewildered by such treatment; many felt they had simply done their duty and did not understand the hostility with which they were greeted. In addition, many veterans were psychologically scarred from their time in Vietnam. Seeing their friends killed or wounded was very traumatic, as was having to be constantly alert for an enemy who could sneak up and kill them. Many veterans relived the horrors of war in nightmares and flashbacks and were still experiencing them years after their return. They suffered from post-traumatic stress, a syndrome common among people who have experienced severe shock or trauma. Others withdrew into a drug- or alcohol-induced haze, the only way they felt they could cope with their problems.

It was not until the 1980s that Vietnam veterans began to earn the respect of their country for their service. A memorial was built for the more than 58,000 Americans who were killed during the war. The country seemed to realize how it had mistreated its veterans and started to come together and begin its healing process.

# Notes

1. Quoted in Stanley Karnow, *Vietnam: A History*. Rev. and updated edition. New York: Penguin, 1997, p. 146.

2. Quoted in Karnow, *Vietnam*, p. 184.

3. Quoted in Peter Macdonald, *Giap: The Victor in Vietnam*. New York: Norton, 1993, p. 126.

4. Quoted in Theodore C. Sorensen, ed., *"Let the Word Go Forth": The Speeches, Statements, and Writings of John F. Kennedy, 1947 to 1963*. New York: Laurel, 1991, p. 12.

5. Quoted in Sorensen, *"Let the Word Go Forth,"* pp. 375–76.

6. Quoted in Karnow, *Vietnam*, p. 411.

7. Quoted in William Appleman Williams et al., eds., *America in Vietnam: A Documentary History*. New York: Norton, 1989, p. 237.

8. Quoted in Robert D. Schulzinger, *A Time for War: The United States and Vietnam 1941–1975*. New York: Oxford University Press, 1997, p. 170.

9. Quoted in Vaughn Davis Bornet, *The Presidency of Lyndon B. Johnson*. Lawrence: University Press of Kansas, 1988, p. 84.

10. Quoted in Karnow, *Vietnam*, p. 481.

11. William C. Westmoreland, *A Soldier Reports*. Garden City, NY: Doubleday, 1976, p. 321.

12. Westmoreland, *A Soldier Reports*, p. 321.

13. Quoted in Williams et al., *America in Vietnam*, p. 275.

14. Quoted in Schulzinger, *A Time for War*, p. 286.

15. Quoted in Schulzinger, *A Time for War*, p. 288.

16. Quoted in Karnow, *Vietnam*, p. 666.

17. Quoted in Karnow, *Vietnam*, p. 669.

18. Quoted in Larry Engelmann, ed., *Tears Before the Rain: An Oral History of the Fall of South Vietnam*. New York: Oxford University Press, 1990, p. 300.

# Chapter 1

# The War at Home

# Chapter Preface

When President Lyndon B. Johnson began escalating American involvement in Vietnam in 1964 and 1965, most Americans supported his decision, and by extension, the war. They had trust and faith in their government to do the correct thing, which in Vietnam meant fighting communism. Many young men volunteered for military service so that they could fight for their country in Vietnam. Some believed it was their duty to serve and they were proud of the opportunity to do so.

As the Vietnam War dragged on, however, more and more Americans began to oppose America's participation in what they considered a civil war. By 1967 and 1968, antiwar protests were attracting thousands of participants in cities across the United States. Protesters argued that the United States had no strategic interests in Vietnam. They believed that the fall of South Vietnam to the Communist-supported Viet Cong would have no effect on the security of the United States.

There were ways—legal and illegal—that men could avoid fighting in Vietnam. Some men went to college. College students could get a deferment from being drafted for four years while they were in school. Some men evaded the draft by having their family physician write a letter stating to the draft board that they were physically unfit for service. Others tried to fake a disability—usually mental illness—to avoid induction. Some men agreed to be drafted but insisted that their moral or religious beliefs prevented them from fighting in the armed forces. These men were classified by the military as conscientious objectors (COs). Sometimes COs were permitted to avoid military duty altogether; others were allowed to serve as noncombatants, such as clerks, truck drivers, and chaplains.

The most drastic step taken by men who refused to fight in Vietnam was to flee the country. These draft dodgers often went to Canada to live. This action made them criminals under U.S. law, and they could be arrested and imprisoned if they ever returned to the United States. Of all the protesters against the war, draft dodgers evoked the most contempt among Vietnam veterans, their families, and those who believed the war in Vietnam was just. They also considered war protesters and conscientious objectors as cowards and traitors. Men and fathers who had served in World War II or Korea could not understand the younger generation's reluctance to do their duty in Vietnam.

# Thoughts About Induction

Tim O'Brien

> By April 1968, nearly half of the American people had grave
> doubts about the morality and rightness of the war in Viet-
> nam. Support for the war had been steadily slipping for two
> years. Protests against the Vietnam War occurred frequently,
> often on college campuses. Although students were able to
> defer their induction while they attended school, they were
> some of the most vocal protesters against the war. During this
> turbulent time, Tim O'Brien graduated from college and soon
> received his induction notice, his official orders to report for
> duty in the Army.
>
> Until the last minute, O'Brien was unsure of whether he
> would report for duty. He believed the war in Vietnam was
> wrong and that Americans were dying there needlessly. Yet, he
> also realized he would disgrace his parents and himself if he
> avoided the draft by going to Canada. All these thoughts and
> more went through his mind as he waited for summer to end.
>
> O'Brien is the author of several books about Vietnam,
> including *Going After Cacciato*, *The Things They Carried*,
> and *If I Die in a Combat Zone: Box Me Up and Ship Me
> Home*, from which this essay is excerpted.

The summer of 1968, the summer I turned into a soldier,
was a good time for talking about war and peace. [Pres-
idential candidate] Eugene McCarthy was bringing quiet
thought to the subject. He was winning votes in the pri-

Excerpted from *If I Die in a Combat Zone: Box Me Up and Ship Me Home*, by Tim
O'Brien. Copyright © 1969, 1970, 1972, 1973 by Tim O'Brien. Reprinted by permission
of Dell Publishing, a division of Random House, Inc.

maries. College students were listening to him, and some of us tried to help out. Lyndon Johnson was almost forgotten, no longer forbidding or feared; Robert Kennedy was dead but not quite forgotten; Richard Nixon looked like a loser. With all the tragedy and change that summer, it was fine weather for discussion.

And, with all of this, there was an induction notice tucked into a corner of my billfold.

## Discussions

So with friends and acquaintances and townspeople, I spent the summer in Fred's antiseptic cafe, drinking coffee and mapping out arguments on Fred's napkins. Or I sat in Chic's tavern, drinking beer with kids from the farms. I played some golf and tore up the pool table down at the bowling alley, keeping an eye open for likely-looking high school girls.

Late at night, the town deserted, two or three of us would drive a car around and around the town's lake, talking about the war, very seriously, moving with care from one argument to the next, trying to make it a dialogue and not a debate. We covered all the big questions: justice, tyranny, self-determination, conscience and the state, God and war and love.

College friends came to visit: "Too bad. I hear you're drafted. What will you do?"

I said I didn't know, that I'd let time decide. Maybe something would change, maybe the war would end. Then we'd turn to discuss the matter, talking long, trying out the questions, sleeping late in the mornings.

The summer conversations, spiked with plenty of references to the philosophers and academicians of war, were thoughtful and long and complex and careful. But, in the end, careful and precise argumentation hurt me. It was painful to tread deliberately over all the axioms and assumptions and corollaries when the people on the town's draft board were calling me to duty, smiling so nicely.

"It won't be bad at all," they said "Stop in and see us

when it's over."

So to bring the conversations to a focus and also to try out in real words my secret fears, I argued for running away.

## The Arguments

I was persuaded then, and I remain persuaded now, that the war was wrong. And since it was wrong and since people were dying as a result of it, it was evil. Doubts, of course, hedged all this: I had neither the expertise nor the wisdom to synthesize answers; the facts were clouded; there was no certainty as to the kind of government that would follow a North Vietnamese victory or, for that matter, an American victory, and the specifics of the conflict were hidden away— partly in men's minds, partly in the archives of government, and partly in buried, irretrievable history. The war, I thought, was wrongly conceived and poorly justified. But perhaps I was mistaken, and who really knew, anyway?

Piled on top of this was the town, my family, my teachers, a whole history of the prairie. Like magnets, these things pulled in one direction or the other, almost physical forces weighting the problem, so that, in the end, it was less reason and more gravity that was the final influence.

My family was careful that summer. The decision was mine and it was not talked about. The town lay there, spread out in the corn and watching me, the mouths of old women and Country Club men poised in readiness to find fault. It was not a town, not a Minneapolis or New York, where the son of a father can sometimes escape scrutiny. More, I owed the prairie something. For twenty-one years I'd lived under its laws, accepted its education, eaten its food, wasted and guzzled its water, slept well at night, driven across its highways, dirtied and breathed its air, wallowed in its luxuries. I'd played on its Little League teams. I remembered Plato's *Crito,* when Socrates, facing certain death—execution, not war—had the chance to escape. But he reminded himself that he had seventy years in which he could have left the country, if he were not satisfied or felt the agreements he'd made with it were unfair. He had not chosen Sparta or Crete.

And, I reminded myself, I hadn't thought much about Canada until that summer.

The summer passed this way. Golden afternoons on the golf course, an illusive hopefulness that the war would grant me a last-minute reprieve, nights in the pool hall or drug store, talking with towns-folk, turning the questions over and over, being a philosopher.

## Time to Go

Near the end of that summer the time came to go to the war. The family indulged in a cautious sort of Last Supper together, and afterward my father, who is brave, said it was time to report at the bus depot. I moped down to my bedroom and looked the place over, feeling quite stupid, thinking that my mother would come in there in a day or two and probably cry a little. I trudged back up to the kitchen and put my satchel down. Everyone gathered around, saying so long and good health and write and let us know if you want anything. My father took up the induction papers, checking on times and dates and all the last-minute things, and when I pecked my mother's face and grabbed the satchel for comfort, he told me to put it down, that I wasn't supposed to report until tomorrow. I'd misread the induction date.

After laughing about the mistake, after a flush of red color and a flood of ribbing and a wave of relief had come and gone, I took a long drive around the lake. Sunset Park, with its picnic table and little beach and a brown wood shelter and some families swimming. The Crippled Children's School. Slater Park, more kids. A long string of split level houses, painted every color.

The war and my person seemed like twins as I went around the town's lake. Twins grafted together and forever together, as if a separation would kill them both.

The thought made me angry.

## Anger

In the basement of my house I found some scraps of cardboard. I printed obscene words on them. I declared my intention to have no part of Vietnam. With delightful vicious-ness, a secret will, I declared the war evil, the draft board evil, the town evil in its lethargic acceptance of it all. For many minutes, making up the signs, making up my mind, I was outside the town. I was outside the law. I imagined my-self strutting up and down the sidewalks outside the depot, the bus waiting and the driver blaring his horn, the *Daily Globe* photographer trying to push me into line with the other draftees, the frantic telephone calls, my head buzzing at the deed.

On the cardboard, my strokes of bright red were big and ferocious looking. The language was clear and certain and burned with a hard, defiant, criminal, blasphemous sound. I tried reading it aloud. I was scared. I was sad.

Later in the evening I tore the signs into pieces and put the shreds in the garbage can outside. I went back into the basement. I slipped the crayons into their box, the same stubs of color I'd used a long time before to chalk in reds and greens on Roy Rogers' cowboy boots.

I'd never been a demonstrator, except in the loose sense. True, I'd taken a stand in the school newspaper on the war, trying to show why it seemed wrong. But, mostly, I'd just listened.

"No war is worth losing your life for," a college acquain-tance used to argue. "The issue isn't a moral one. It's a mat-ter of efficiency: What's the most efficient way to stay alive when your nation is at war? That's the issue."

But others argued that no war is worth losing your coun-try for, and when asked about the case when a country fights a wrong war, those people just shrugged.

Most of my college friends found easy paths away from the problem, all to their credit. Deferments for this and that. Letters from doctors or chaplains. It was hard to find people who had to think much about the problem. Counsel came from two main quarters, pacifists and veterans of foreign wars, but neither camp had much to offer. It wasn't a matter of peace, as the pacifists argued, but rather a matter of when and when not to join others in making war. And it wasn't a matter of listening to an ex-lieutenant colonel talk about serving in a right war, when the question was whether to serve in what seemed a wrong one.

On August 13, I went to the bus depot. A Worthington [Minnesota] *Daily Globe* photographer took my picture standing by a rail fence with four other draftees.

Then the bus took us through corn fields, to little towns along the way—Rushmore and Adrian—where other recruits came aboard. With the tough guys drinking beer and howling in the back seats, brandishing their empty cans and calling one another "scum" and "trainee" and "GI Joe," with all this noise and hearty farewelling, we went to Sioux Falls: We spent the night in a YMCA. I went out alone for a beer, drank it in a corner booth, then I bought a book and read it in my room.

## Submission

At noon the next day our hands were in the air, even the tough guys. We recited the oath—some of us loudly and daringly, others in bewilderment. It was a brightly lighted room, wood paneled. A flag gave the place the right colors. There was smoke in the air. We said the words, and we were soldiers.

I'd never been much of a fighter. I was afraid of bullies: frustrated anger. Still, I deferred to no one. Positively lorded myself over inferiors. And on top of that was the matter of conscience and conviction, uncertain and surface-deep but pure nonetheless. I was a confirmed liberal. Not a pacifist, but I would have cast my ballot to end the Vietnam war, I would have voted for Eugene McCarthy, hoping he would make peace. I was not soldier material, that was certain.

But I submitted. All the soul searchings and midnight conversations and books and beliefs were voided by abstention, extinguished by forfeiture, for lack of oxygen, by a sort of sleepwalking default. It was no decision, no chain of ideas or reasons, that steered me into the war.

It was an intellectual and physical stand-off, and I did not have the energy to see it to an end. I did not want to be a soldier, not even an observer to war. But neither did I want to upset a peculiar balance between the order I knew, the people I knew, and my own private world. It was not just that I valued that order. I also feared its opposite—inevitable chaos, censure, embarrassment, the end of everything that had happened in my life, the end of it all.

And the stand-off is still there. I would wish this book [O'Brien's book] could take the form of a plea for everlasting peace, a plea from one who knows, from one who's been there and come back, an old soldier looking back at a dying war.

That would be good. It would be fine to integrate it all to persuade my younger brother and perhaps some others to say no to wrong wars.

Or it would be fine to confirm the old beliefs about war: It's horrible, but it's a crucible of men and events and, in the end, it makes more of a man out of you.

But, still, none of this seems right.

## Truths

Now, war ended, all I am left with are simple, unprofound straps of truth. Men die. Fear hurts and humiliates. It is hard to be brave. It is hard to know what bravery *is*. Dead human beings are heavy and awkward to carry, things smell different in Vietnam, soldiers are dreamers, drill sergeants are boors, some men thought the war was proper and others didn't and most didn't care. Is that the stuff for a morality lesson, even for a theme?

Do dreams offer lessons? Do nightmares have themes, do we awaken and analyze them and live our lives and advise others as a result? Can the foot soldier teach anything important about war, merely for having been there? I think not. He can tell war stories.

# Draft Dodger

Ron Stone

Congress re-instituted the draft—a forced conscription into the armed forces—in 1948, and it was continued until 1971. Of the 26,800,000 men of draft age during the Vietnam War, almost 16 million never served in the military because of deferments, disqualifications, or exemptions. About 570,000 of those were draft dodgers, those who purposely evaded the draft in one way or another. Many of these young men fled to Canada.

Ron Stone is an example of a draft dodger who went to Canada to avoid going to Vietnam. Before he was drafted, Stone worked fulltime as an aide to the U.S. Senate Majority Leader while he was attending college. When Stone received his draft notice in 1969, he knew he would not fight in a war which he felt was wrong. Stone refused to report and left for Canada instead. He lived in Canada for seven years eluding notices from his draft board to report, the police, and the FBI. In 1975, the federal case against him for evading the draft was dropped, and Stone returned to the United States. He moved to West Hollywood, California, where he continued his political career. He is known as the "Father of West Hollywood" for his role in the city's affairs. He died in 1988. Sherry Gottlieb is a freelance writer who interviewed Stone for her book *Hell No, We Won't Go! Resisting the Draft During the Vietnam War,* from which this essay is taken.

I'd always been politically active—since about the fourth grade. When John Kennedy ran for President in 1960, I

Excerpted from "The Expatriates," by Ron Stone, in *Hell No We Won't Go: Resisting the Draft During the Vietnam War*, edited by Sherry Gershon Gottlieb (New York: Viking, 1991). Copyright © Sherry Gershon Gottlieb, 1991. Reprinted with permission from Sherry Gershon Gottlieb.

was somewhat of an expert on military strategy and military hardware; in the eighth grade, I'd read every book around on nuclear force deployments, strategic theory—I knew all the latest weapons technologies.

In 1964, I was appointed to be a page boy in the U.S. Senate by Senator Paul Douglas of Illinois. I was on the floor of the Senate from the beginning of the American involvement in the war in Vietnam. . . .

## The War Picks Up

In the summer of 1966, the war had picked up, the U.S. was rolling strongly. I was at the first International Summer School at Cambridge University, and I had pretty much been sold on the success of the war effort. It seemed like progress was being made, and the bad guys were being pushed back to where they belonged. I was the most supportive I ever was of the Vietnam effort during that time overseas. I felt pretty much forced to defend my country against every other country [represented] there. I remember being embarrassed later for the questions I asked that summer of members of the British government.

I graduated from Page School and had become an aide to the Majority Leader in the Democratic Cloak Room, which is the inner sanctum of the Senate. Only Senators were allowed in the room, with the exception of the three majority assistants, of which I was one. It's really the nerve center of the Senate. It's where all the top discussion takes place, and it's also the telephone communication [center] between the Senate and the outside world, including their offices.

Meanwhile, Vietnam is getting worse; more and more troops are going there. I'm starting to realize that the situation is the quagmire that everyone's called it all along. The opposition is starting to grow. Robert Kennedy was starting to get very critical, in private, of the war in Vietnam. The intellectuals of the East Coast had become very critical in their writings. I was at George Washington University, where speakers were raising our consciousness about Vietnam during civil rights rallies. Richard Barnet comes to mind. His thinking was so logical and so clear: he talked about how the Vietnam War was not a war against Vietnamese as much as a war against our whole system, and against ourselves. That really sunk into me. I [became] the most left-wing member of the Majority staff

## Anti-War Demonstrations

The airlines had introduced youth fares, and [since] I found it easier to keep my pace going on the weekends, I flew all over the country. I was the youngest member of the hundred-thousand-mile club on three different airlines. I went to demonstrations, including, in Philadelphia, the first public demonstration against the war in Vietnam. It brought the point home to me, and I took the message back to the Senate floor. Whenever there was an incident anywhere, I would be there: a student rebellion at Harvard, the storming of Dartmouth. People's Park in Berkeley. (One of the great disappointments of my life was not being on Nixon's enemy list.) I had a good feeling that there was unrest out there, and things were changing, although, clearly, it wasn't the majority. The lines got drawn closer and closer. People were choosing up sides on Vietnam—it was like the Civil War all over again. It was dividing families and friends—people were very passionate about it.

In the summer of 1967, I went to Montreal for the world's fair. Expo '67 was the greatest thing that happened in the history of Man, the highest watermark of human civilization. It was the best that every country had to offer. Canada was so impressive that you just couldn't help but be stunned by how far ahead the culture was to anything I was living in, even though I was at the top of American culture—at least in the sense of having a perspective on what was going on, access to information. [Expo '67] left such a positive impression in my mind about Canada.

It was my job as a member of the Majority staff to predict votes, and try to provide a sense of perspective on how legislation was progressing. In the Senate, it was my firm conviction that we had enough votes to stop the war by cutting off appropriations. It would have been as close as a one- or two-vote margin. Robert Kennedy was the moral supporter of the issue. There was a rumbling of dissatisfaction with Mike Mansfield as Majority Leader that grew out of the frustration that the Senators were feeling having to deal with the passion of the Vietnam issue. Vietnam somehow never got to the point where it could be voted one way or the other.

We were approaching the Presidential election in 1968. The first salvo that was officially thrown in the effort was Robert Kennedy's speech in Chicago: he made a vicious attack on the Vietnam War—the first public statement that any major leader in the Democratic Party had made against the war, which gave me the freedom to start speaking more openly, too. I had become pretty close to Robert Kennedy. I had a reputation for being the only person who could get through to him when he was in serious meditation. We had an excellent relationship, and I spent many weekends at the house, playing touch football and swimming, going to parties.

## The Pressure Grows

At the same time, pressure was growing on me. I was in my junior year in school, studying foreign relations; courses were getting tough. If you don't keep your grade-point average up, you're going to get drafted. I was one of the people who strongly argued that the draft should be made egalitarian, that it shouldn't just be a poor people's army; we ought to get rid of college deferments and make everybody subject to the draft. I still strongly feel that that was the right position. While I was able to help push that policy through the Senate, it came back to haunt me: I was one of the people upon whom that pressure was falling. I had to keep my grades up. I kept going to school full-time, and working sixty hours a week on the Senate floor, under enormous pressure.

I left the Cloak Room and went to work as a lobbyist for American Airlines, which reduced my hours and allowed me to keep my schoolwork afloat. I very much continued to stay involved in politics. I was still going to parties at

Robert Kennedy's house, and still traveling all over the country to demonstrations, and in many ways was more outspoken than before. I certainly hadn't lost any of my contacts in the Senate.

Then, June 5, 1968, at the Ambassador Hotel [Robert Kennedy's assassination], my world just collapsed, just completely collapsed. I had invested all my eggs in the basket of that wing of the Democratic Party gaining control, not just of the party, but of the country. The service at St. Patrick's, and the funeral train, was just devastating—I'm not sure I've recovered even now. I certainly can't talk about the trip without going to tears. I really lost a lot of faith in the political process, which probably wasn't justified on the basis of one event. I really became disillusioned in a hurry. I just couldn't support [presidential candidate] Hubert Humphrey's "happy warrior" approach—we had a war going on, there was nothing to be happy about. The war itself was just becoming a horrendous mess. Clearly, we were being pinned back against the wall. Nixon's victory was the last straw for me. I knew Nixon personally; he used to stand outside the Cloak Room door all the time. I'm not saying I loathed the man, but I didn't have any respect at all for his politics. He was the epitome of evil for a left-wing Democrat.

When Nixon had control of the government, things just went from bad to worse. I regret now that I didn't work harder for Humphrey. By then, the counterculture had grown into a fully supportive, integrated cross-ethic of people who smoked dope, were against the war, for free sex—all these things tied individual opinions together. I even had a ponytail then—now you can barely see my hairline!

I let it be known to everyone that there was absolutely no way I was going to serve in Nixon's army, and there was absolutely no way I was going to serve in Vietnam. I did everything I had to do as a college student to stay out of the draft—I kept my course load up, I kept my grades up, I took the tests that you had to take. But, even having worked as hard as I did to get through college, I was still a couple of courses short of graduating with the rest of my class in

1969. The draft board wouldn't let me go the extra semester to finish college—they said, "That's it—you've had your four years." I did everything I could to delay it, transferring [draft] boards—everyone knew all these tricks for delaying—from suburban Chicago to the Virginia suburbs of Washington. That got me another month or two, and eventually they said, "It's time for your physical." I was still trying to stay in college, still trying to get my courses done; but it just collapsed around Christmas 1969.

I proposed to my girlfriend, saying, "Why don't we go live in Canada?" That was more than she could handle. I lost my girl. The college career had come to an end with the draft. I had no work at that point. I decided to go to Canada.

## Canada

I reserved a flight from O'Hare Airport in Chicago to Toronto via Air Canada, under a different name. Once at O'Hare, I went immediately up to the hundred-thousand-mile club and hid out up there until the very last minute, then rushed down to catch the flight. An hour and a half later, we were landing in Toronto.

Customs was very tense; I just said I was there on business and walked right through. Free at last! I wanted to kiss the ground. I got on the bus to go downtown, not really knowing where I was going to go. I had a hundred and fifty dollars and I was owed another three hundred dollars on my tax refund that was going to be sent to my parents. On the way downtown, I asked a guy from the same flight if he knew where the Y was; he said he was from St. Louis, visiting his girlfriend. I told him I was a draft dodger, and he said his girlfriend might be able to help; so the first person I met in Canada who helped me out was an American. I slept on their couch for a couple of days before I got a room in a rooming house.

The next day, I went to the agency which helped draft dodgers in Toronto. The head guy was a classic old-time Socialist, and he offered advice about how hopeless my situation was: how it was unlikely I'd find a job at all, how slim

the chances were that Immigration would grant me resi-
dency, that it was so hopeless that I'd better turn back. He
told me you had to get so many "points" to become a
"landed immigrant," and of the difficulty of finding a job
without landed immigrant status . . . but that it was impossible to get landed immigrant status without a job.

I was going to have to deal with my parents if I was going to eat, because they had my tax refund. That led to a
very tense call, but they did agree to forward it.

Everywhere I went for work in Toronto was an American
subsidiary, and there was no way they were going to hire
me. The strictly Canadian firms didn't want an immigrant.
This went on for about three months. I got very sick and
nearly died. I finally decided to move to Vancouver to be
closer to my girlfriend in San Francisco. I spent seventy-six
of my last hundred dollars on a train ticket to Vancouver,
leaving me twenty-four dollars upon arrival.

## Moving to Vancouver

I did the whole thing over again with the agency in Vancouver. The people in Vancouver, unlike Toronto, had organized through the Unitarian Church to house draft dodgers.
[They] had developed an underground railway system to
help people get established by providing them with food and
shelter in one-week intervals. Every week I would be shifted
to another home. I had come to realize that Vancouver was
a very special place. I did all sorts of odd jobs, a dollar here
and there under the table.

I had to get landed immigrant status, for which I needed
a job offer. It was clear to me that the only thing I could do
was to create a corporation that would write me a job offer.
I started the first direct-charge food co-op in British Co-
lumbia, for the Unitarian Church. When the organization
was established enough to afford stationery, its Chairman of
the Board (whom I had appointed) wrote me a job offer.

Then he and his wife drove me to the airport in Seattle,
an enormously nerve-racking experience, so that I could "arrive" in Canada—you couldn't become a landed immigrant

from within the country. They dropped me off at the airport and then drove back to Vancouver to pick me up when I landed. I again hid in the hundred-thousand-mile club until the last minute, when I went down to the gate to stand by for the flight. While I was waiting at gate 6, there was an announcement over the intercom: "Airport security—gate 6!" I was sitting at gate 6 . . . there's nothing going on here. What's the problem? Oh, shit, maybe it's *me*. Then: "FBI—gate 6." Oh my God, it's over, they've got me now. I sat there smoking a cigar, trying to act as cool as possible. There were only three or four people sitting there. This classic narc sort of person went to the gate attendant, and they had a few words, and she gets on the speaker and calls my name. I go up to the counter, thinking it's all over, and she gives me my ticket. I get on the plane. Finally it fills and they close the door. The narc type and another agent walk down the center aisle of the plane, staring everybody in the eye. They finally leave, and the plane taxis to the end of the runway. Then the pilot came over the speaker and said, "I'm sorry. There's absolutely nothing wrong with the plane, but we've been ordered back to the gate." We went back to the gate, the door opens, and the same two guys got back on the plane again and took a more careful look. They were really looking hard for someone. Finally they left, and the plane took off. [I looked so panicked that] the guy next to me said, "Son, I can tell you've never flown before, but don't worry—it'll be all right."

## Interrogation

Arriving in Vancouver was much more laid back than Toronto—except when I got to the point where they said, "How long do you plan to stay?" etc. I said, "I want to apply for permanent landed immigrant status." I'd purposely picked a Sunday afternoon as the least likely day for security in the States. They sent me to a side room, where they were surprised that I had all the proper papers. It turned into a Nazi war movie, where they sat me down at a desk, and they had a bright light shining in my eyes, and they grilled me for about three hours. Serious interrogation—questions on how I got the job offer, where I worked before, was I sure I hadn't been in Canada before, did I ever use drugs. The support of my employer, my arguments, and the fact that it was Sunday and an awkward situation to begin with, they ended up letting me in the country. I really didn't think they were going to—right up to the end, I thought they were going to send me back. On the same flight I'd arrived on, fifteen draft dodgers were sent back to Seattle.

With my landed immigrant status, I could look for work. Two months later, I found a job as a dishwasher in a hospital, at a dollar thirty-five an hour. I moved up to gardener. Later I helped reorganize an insurance agency, started getting into my old line of work, managing and consulting on organization.

## Constant Harassment

There was constant harassment of my family by the FBI—they knew damn well I was in Vancouver, but they would arrive at my family's house at two and three A.M. and bang on the door and wake them up and demand to see whether or not I was living there. They did that for years. My family didn't even tell me about it for a year or two, they were so embarrassed by it.

I drove down to San Francisco in 1970 to visit my girlfriend and stayed in California for a few days. While I was there, someone came to the door who looked like a narc, which got everyone suspicious. Two hours later, the police arrived suddenly from all directions and completely surrounded the building. I ran from the apartment, up the stairs to the roof, to escape. The worst thing about being a draft dodger is the dreams that you have for years of being chased. It turned out to be a false fire alarm for the building across the street. The next day, I went back to Vancouver.

I spent seven years in Canada. In 1975, there was a lawyer in Milwaukee who was researching cases in Chicago that might be dismissed for technicalities; my case was being prosecuted in Chicago as a model case. The lawyer found a technicality in my case that was so serious, there was no way they could prosecute me, and he was willing to proceed with the case for twelve hundred dollars. It turns out that they had sent my actual induction notice to my address in Toronto and it sat on the step there for months, and had finally been returned to them unopened. It was in my file in Chicago. There was the proof that I had not received my induction notice. They had no case. We won, and I got a letter from the FBI saying the case had been dismissed and that there were no other warrants for my arrest.

In all honesty, I don't think I've had any further repercussions. People have generally respected the fact that I made a decision on an important issue. I've been active in West Hollywood [California] politics to the point where I'm the father of the city. I have a plaque from the city council, thanking me for my services in having founded and led the cityhood effort here. I've run for city council twice.

# Conscientious Objector

David Brown

Not all those who avoided the draft were college students or draft dodgers. Some who were against the war were conscientious objectors (COs), men who were opposed to participation in war. Many COs would agree to perform noncombatant military service (such as a medic, cook, truck driver, or chaplain's aide) or alternative civilian service, usually in hospitals, government agencies, or nonprofit organizations, instead of being trained for armed combat.

For men who were not Quakers or Mennonites (traditional pacifist religions) getting the government to approve their status as a conscientious objector sometimes proved difficult. Applicants wishing to be designated a conscientious objector had to fill out forms which asked detailed questions about their religious beliefs and when they believed the use of force could be justified. An applicant did not have much recourse if his CO application was denied by the government. David Brown is a conscientious objector who continued his fight against the army even when his CO application was denied not once, but twice. He refused to obey orders to train, even to dress in combat fatigues, and was imprisoned, court-martialed, dishonorably discharged, and imprisoned again. Yet his belief that the Vietnam War was wrong never wavered. Gerald R. Gioglio is the author of *Days of Decision: An Oral History of Conscientious Objectors in the Military During the Vietnam War*, in which this selection appears.

Excerpted from David Brown's account in *Days of Decision: An Oral History of Conscientious Objectors in the Military During the Vietnam War*, edited by Gerald R. Gioglio (Trenton, NJ: Broken Rifle Press, 1989). Copyright © 1989 Gerald R. Gioglio. Reprinted with permission.

Once I decided I couldn't participate in the military anymore, I just told them, "I'm not going to fall out for basic training tomorrow." But, after a day of communication and confrontation, the drill sergeant convinced me that the first couple of weeks were just first aid and map reading; so, I gave it a chance.

## Filing for CO Status

Meanwhile, my wife discovered and contacted the Central Committee for Conscientious Objectors. They sent me a copy of the discharge regulations, the *Handbook for Conscientious Objectors* and their memo on CO discharges. I had been going through the training program and attending the lectures, and the obscenity of it all became clearer and clearer. So, I went to the orderly room and told them I wanted to apply for discharge as a CO. I'm not sure how I was able to do this, because I had no prior experience in confronting authority. It was a tense time. They tried to grab the paperwork out of my hands like it was classified information or something. But, I managed to convince them to allow me to apply for discharge.

I thought that while I filled out the CO forms I wouldn't have to continue with basic; but they decided I had to complete the paperwork first, then I would be removed from basic training. So, I was stuck with another couple of weeks of basic while trying to write the application in my spare time. I really wanted to complete the forms by the beginning of the fifth week, because that was when we were going to the rifle range.

I handed in a handwritten application, but they said it had to be typed! They consented to have it typed, but still wouldn't pull me out of training. So, I ended up having to go off to the rifle range. Finally, they brought my paperwork out to be signed. Well, the company clerk, damn his hide, had decided that I had given him more than he was willing to type; so, he reduced it to a very badly done outline. I was left with the choice of either signing this hash or continuing with the training. So, I just signed it, and the application I wrote was not officially presented to the Army.

I was removed from basic training and assigned to permanent KP. However, the first sergeant knew I was a good typist and pulled me into the orderly room. So, from the day after I was pulled out of basic training, until my first discharge request was denied, I functioned as a company clerk.

As graduation time approached I tracked down my application, and found that it had not left the post. They were trying to pretend that nothing had happened. They even gave me advanced training orders to report to Fort Benjamin Harrison to learn to be a stenographer. They just kept the application as a way to deal with me. But, I knew I was not going anywhere. I was determined to get out. In my mind I was giving the Army a chance to follow its own rules. I told them to cancel the orders and to process my CO application.

I came to realize that every job in the military was dictated by the needs of combat. Everything in the military is a combat support function. There isn't a job that is not combat support. Even a chaplain's assistant fires a weapon. It's part of the job; it's part of everybody's job. It's your first job. You're in the infantry first and then you do whatever else you're doing. It was absolutely clear that that's what the organization was about. Period.

## Back into Basic Training

My application came back denied. So, they put me back into basic at the approximate point where I was removed. I made it clear from the minute I hit the place that I was not going to train. I fell out with everybody, but I didn't even do the Physical Training. I was threatened by the squad leader, I got yelled at and called names, but I stayed cool and just stood there.

That evening they tried to get me to draw a rifle. The sergeant tried to hand it to me, but I did not put out my hands to catch it; I let it fall to the floor. At this point, I think he knew I was serious, because none of those guys wanted anything to happen to those weapons. Then, I refused a direct order to take the weapon. That was tense. I just screwed

up the courage and faced it. I tried to be clear, said very little, just "No." I expected to get clobbered at any minute, but
I wasn't. Being called names didn't bother me particularly;
it was, like, part of the game. I just closed myself off to it.

They isolated me, like some kind of scum, moved me out
of the squad bay to a room where nobody else was. In fact,
they got me out of the company within thirty-six hours. I
was sent to a holding company to await court-martial. That
was tense, too; going to the stockade wasn't really high on
my list. About a week later I got a special court-martial.
There wasn't much to say, in fact, I was advised not to say
anything at all—a "keep silent defense." At that point my
position was to just get through it. I wasn't raising any issues; so, I didn't make a statement. They sentenced me to
three months in the stockade.

Then, the brigade commander wanted to speak to me. He
gave me the "fatherly talk." He said, "I'm going to assign
you to a basic training company that has never heard of you.
I'll suspend your sentence and give you another chance." I
told him it was hopeless, but he reassigned me anyway.

As soon as I got to the new basic training unit I told them,
"I'm not going to train, forget it, don't bother." The captain
ordered me to go sign out a rifle, and gave me an hour to do
it. So I went back to the barracks, and an hour later I was
called to the orderly room. He charged me with disobeying
a direct order and sent me back to the holding company.

By this time I was getting some help; the American Civil
Liberties Union had decided to take my case. The Army also
gave me an excellent Judge Advocate attorney, he actually
did the job I needed done—he got the charges dropped. It
turns out the company commander didn't have any evidence. He just believed me when I told him I never checked
out a weapon. They never called anyone in from the supply
room to see if I had been there. Nobody even knew me, so
they couldn't testify as to whether or not I had complied. So,
there was no evidence and the charge was dropped. But, that
led to my suspended sentence being lifted. And one day, after just giving blood at the bloodmobile, I came back to find

out that I was on my way to the stockade. It was the week before Thanksgiving, that was a real kick in the pants. . . .

## Petition Denied

We petitioned federal court for a habeas corpus, on the grounds that I was a conscientious objector and the Army, by refusing to recognize my status, was holding me illegally. On the day of the hearing, which was held in Trenton, New Jersey, I had to pack all my stuff and leave the stockade barracks. I spent the day in a holding cell. The Army thought the judge might rule in my favor; so, they were preparing me for release. Finally, at four or five o'clock in the afternoon, the order came that I wasn't being released after all. The petition was denied and I was returned to the cellblock. That was worse than being put in the stockade in the first place. It was a real low point, I was frustrated as hell.

I did the rest of my time, and was released from the stockade in January 1967. Whereupon, wonder of wonders, the Army expected me to continue with basic training! This time they took me to the supply section, and again I refused to draw my gear. They threatened to give me another direct order and to send me back to the stockade. I simply said, "Send me back." It was getting tiresome.

## Another CO Application

I went back to the barracks to pack for the stockade. But, lo and behold, I got called back to the orderly room. They said, "We suggest that you apply for a CO discharge again and we'll recommend that it be approved. We think you're sincere."

This time I was able to put together a good package. But, it took forever for a decision to come back. I applied in January and I didn't hear anything until the end of May 1967. It was a long, long winter and I was getting real antsy about it. I was still in the Army; I was very aware that, even where I was, I was doing a job for the Army. I was explicitly not willing to do that, it was not where I belonged. I became especially aware of wearing the uniform and what that symbolized. By wearing it I felt I was expressing my support for war; it became very odious. I was seriously considering refusing to wear the uniform; but the ACLU advised me to

---

# The Special Form for Conscientious Objectors

*In order for potential draftees to obtain either 1-O (conscientious objector) or 1-A-O (noncombatant) status from their draft board, the men had to fill out a special form that asked detailed questions about his religious beliefs. The applicants not only had to have good writing skills, but had to express well-developed ideas on war and peace.*

SELECTED QUESTIONS FROM THE SELECTIVE SERVICE SYSTEM'S SPECIAL FORM FOR CONSCIENTIOUS OBJECTORS, SSS Form 150, revised February 10, 1966.

RELIGIOUS TRAINING AND BELIEF

1. Do you believe in a Supreme Being? Yes No.

2. Describe the nature of your belief which is the basis of your claim . . . and state whether or not your belief in a Supreme Being involves duties which to you are superior to those arising from any human relation.

3. Explain how, when, and from whom or from what source you received the training and acquired the belief which is the basis of your claim.

4. Give the name and present address of the individual upon whom you rely most for religious guidance.

5. Under what circumstances, if any do you believe in the use of force?

6. Describe the actions and behavior in your life which in your opinion most conspicuously demonstrate the consistency and depth of your religious convictions.

7. Have you ever given public expression, written or oral, to the views herein expressed as the basis for your claim? If so, specify when and where.

Quoted in Gerald R. Gioglio, *Days of Decision: An Oral History of Conscientious Objectors in the Military During the Vietnam War*, 1989.

wait until a decision was reached on my CO application. So, I waited.

During this time I was reading and becoming more anti-war. For example, around this time the "Fort Hood Three" surfaced. These were the first three guys to publicly refuse orders to go to Vietnam. A journalist from the *Philadelphia Inquirer* came to Fort Dix and interviewed some guys about the Fort Hood Three situation. After the article appeared I wrote the reporter a long letter. I told him some GIs supported the Fort Hood Three and thought they were doing something that was very important. My letter was printed, not as an editorial, but as a feature article in the *Inquirer.* Shortly after that, I was called into the orderly room; the brass was absolutely furious. What really galled them was I had typed the article on their own typewriter, in their own orderly room, and on their own paper.

Eventually, my CO application came back denied. Prior to this, I had prepared a statement saying that if my discharge was denied I was not going to wear the uniform, I was not going to do any work and I was not going to eat. I gave it to the company commander, he looked at it and said, "Go home, I haven't seen this; go home and think about it." So, I went home, called the lawyers and made my plans.

## Refusing to Obey Orders

Originally, I was going to take sanctuary in the chapel. But, that didn't happen. Instead, I wore civilian clothes, the suit I got married in, and appeared before the company commander. He gave me an order to put on a uniform and to report to my usual place of work. I refused. He got his .45 and drove me over to the stockade.

I was not going to do any work, so at workcall, I stayed in the cellblock. An hour or so later the sergeant came through rousting out whoever was there. I refused to go to work. All of a sudden, I found myself face down on the floor with my arms behind my back. It was very quickly and cleanly done; I didn't offer any physical resistance. Then, two or three of them hauled me over to the orderly room.

Then, the stockade commander gave me an order to fall out for workcall. I refused and explained why. So, they took me down to solitary confinement and put me in a cell. Later they called me up, put me in a room with two sergeants and told me I was going to put on a uniform. Again, I said, "No." Well, they got on either side of me, pulled my shirt and ripped it off. They grabbed my waistband and ripped my pants off. Then they got me on the floor and pushed a pair of fatigues and boots on me. I was physically not cooperating; I just went limp on them. So, they just kind of shoved me into the uniform. They cuffed my hands behind my back and took me to the control area to wait for an escort back to solitary. I was determined not to wear that uniform and I managed to wiggle my pants off. There I was standing in the orderly room with my shirt on and my pants around my ankles.

## In Solitary

They led me back to solitary, took the cuffs off and told me to keep the uniform on. They threatened me saying, "If you take that uniform off we'll break your arm." I reached up to unbutton it and again found myself face down. They took my glasses off and put restraining straps on me, leg cuffs, wrist cuffs and a strap to hog-tie me. They picked me up, carried me along the hall, got to my cell and began to swing me, "one—two." Then they stopped, took the mattress off the bunk and swung me again, "one—two," and Lord have mercy, I landed on the bunk. They left me that way for a bunch of hours, until they brought me supper. They said they would untie me if I would agree not to take the uniform off. I told them that was hopeless; so, they said, "Okay, stay the way you are." Sometime that evening they untied me, I guess they figured I didn't have to wear my uniform to sleep. They untied me, I took off my uniform and that was that.

Since I wasn't following their routine they said I couldn't have any of the benefits. They took the mattress, they took my pillow and they took my blankets. I was there with nothing but the metal plate that hung down from the wall for a bunk. That and a New Testament, one of those little pocket deals, which became my pillow. I kept the uniform off for a whole week in spite of the fact that all I had was my briefs. My lawyers were calling, so there was some pressure on them to stop abusing me; they also finally got the message that they had to give me back my blankets.

During this time I was also fasting, water and plain tea, no nourishing liquids; so, they took me up to the medical station every day, in my briefs, to weigh me and to check my vital signs. That was the routine, me hanging out in solitary confinement, doing what reading I could, meditating and getting letters from people I didn't even know. The letters were wonderful. Somebody wrote and asked if she could send curtains for my cell! I felt strong and very, very together.

## In the Hospital

Finally, after twenty-five days, they decided I was beginning to dehydrate and they put me in the hospital. I was under threat of being force-fed; but before that happened, on the twenty-eighth day, I agreed to eat. I rationalized that I did not want to force them to use violence on me. Also, I knew feeding tubes were a wretched experience. I made it clear that if they sent me back to the stockade I was going to stop eating again. As a prisoner, in solitary confinement, I was in a resistance situation, because being there was unjust. They had no right to have me there and I wasn't going to cooperate. In the hospital I was getting medical treatment, because my fasting had dehydrated me; that was okay, I could cooperate.

I spent the summer at the hospital while the Army conducted an investigation that led to my general court-martial. I was charged with refusing an order to put on the uniform, refusing an order to report to work, and for possession of civilian clothes while in trainee status. I was looking at a maximum sentence of fifteen-and-a-half years. However, the ACLU raised a stink about my being assaulted and tied up, and people had organized a demonstration, on my behalf, outside the gates of the base; so, the charges were reduced to a single five year charge of disobeying a direct order.

# Court-Martial

I had four lawyers at my court-martial, three from ACLU and a JAG officer. I stated my case and had a jousting session with the prosecuting attorney. The court-martial panel, of course, found me guilty. There wasn't much to dispute, the orders were given and I didn't follow them. Then they got into sentencing. My parents came in from Chicago and testified, my wife testified, my chaplain testified, and apparently the panel was impressed. They retired to their deliberations and sent back a question; they wanted to know if they could sentence me to a general discharge. Well, the answer was no; so, they gave me eighteen months and a bad conduct discharge.

Being convicted and sentenced made a difference in what I was willing to do. Before this I hadn't been convicted of a crime, I hadn't even gone AWOL. So, I felt it was an injustice for me to be in the stockade. Once I was convicted I agreed to be put to work. I was returned to the stockade and a few months later was transported to Fort Leavenworth, Kansas.

# Federal Prison

Finally, at Fort Leavenworth, I ran into other COs. There were also political prisoners there, people who had refused orders because of opposition to the war in Vietnam. The COs tended to be religious individualists; so, there were fundamental differences and a self-conscious division between the two groups. The COs were putting in their time, the political prisoners were into gaming the system. There wasn't much organizing going on; but, a Unitarian minister came in each Sunday for discussion groups. A lot of the political people attended this.

For me, Leavenworth was a pretty low-key place. The majority of the prisoners were there for AWOL and desertion. It wasn't a heavy scene, but you knew you had to be careful. Everyone, especially if you were not real big, went through a sort of testing to see if you were going to allow yourself to be used sexually. I had to do some fending off and did. But, that soon stopped.

My initial assignment was KP. That lasted for a couple of weeks until they got enough new guys to completely replace our shift. After that, I worked in the mental hygiene section doing screening tests. But, prison time is blank, dead, nothing happening time. The routine is set and things sort of happen to you; you don't make them happen. I read a lot. Before going to prison, I loved to read, but I came to hate it.

I actually got out of prison early; every general court-martial conviction of a year or more automatically got heard by some review board; they reduced my sentence to one year. By the time these machinations were over I had already served more than that. So, I was called in one day and told I was getting out; I left Fort Leavenworth three days later.

# Vietnam Veterans Against the War

John F. Kerry

The Vietnam Veterans Against the War (VVAW) organization was formed in 1967 to protest the war in Vietnam. In February 1971, about 150 members of VVAW met in Detroit to hold hearings about the violence and crimes they committed or witnessed in Vietnam. Although the media paid little attention to this gathering, it paid more attention to their week-long meeting in Washington, DC, in April 1971. Over one thousand VVAW members took part in this meeting, which culminated with a protest on the steps of the U.S. Capitol. There, one by one, they made a statement, then threw their medals for valor and bravery—Bronze Stars, Silver Stars, Purple Hearts—onto the Capitol's steps. Millions of Americans watched this demonstration on television, and President Richard Nixon was unnerved by the veterans' very public antiwar protest.

John F. Kerry, a Navy lieutenant, was representing the VVAW when he spoke to the Senate Foreign Relations Committee a day earlier about the war. He had been awarded the Silver Star, the Bronze Star with oak leaf cluster, and three Purple Hearts. Kerry went on to be elected lieutenant governor of Massachusetts in 1982 and U.S. senator in 1984, 1990, and 1996. Kerry was a naval officer on a gunboat in the Mekong Delta area of Vietnam in 1968–1969. The following selection is a statement he made before the Senate Foreign Relations committee on April 22, 1971.

Excerpted from John F. Kerry's testimony before the U.S. Senate Committee on Foreign Relations, April 22, 1971.

I would like to talk to you a little bit about what the result is of the feelings these men carry with them after coming back from Vietnam. The country doesn't know it yet but it has created a monster, a monster in the form of millions of men who have been taught to deal and to trade in violence and who are given the chance to die for the biggest nothing in history; men who have returned with a sense of anger and a sense of betrayal which no one has yet grasped.

As a veteran and one who feels this anger I would like to talk about it. We are angry because we feel we have been used in the worst fashion by the administration of this country.

In 1970 at West Point Vice President [Spiro] Agnew said "some glamorize the criminal misfits of society while our best men die in Asian rice paddies to preserve the freedom which most of those misfits abuse," and this was used as a rallying point for our effort in Vietnam.

## A Terrible Distortion

But for us, as boys in Asia whom the country was supposed to support, his statement is a terrible distortion from which we can only draw a very deep sense of revulsion, and hence the anger of some of the men who are here in Washington today. It is a distortion because we in no way consider ourselves the best men of this country; because those he calls misfits were standing up for us in a way that nobody else in this country dared to; because so many who have died would have returned to this country to join the misfits in their efforts to ask for an immediate withdrawal from South Vietnam; because so many of those best men have returned as quadriplegics and amputees—and they lie forgotten in Veterans Administration Hospitals in this country which fly the flag which so many have chosen as their own personal symbol—and we cannot consider ourselves America's best men when we are ashamed of and hated for what we were called on to do in Southeast Asia.

In our opinion, and from our experience, there is nothing in South Vietnam which could happen that realistically threatens the United States of America. And to attempt to justify the loss of one American life in Vietnam, Cambodia or Laos by linking such loss to the preservation of freedom, which those misfits supposedly abuse, is to us the height of criminal hypocrisy, and it is that kind of hypocrisy which we feel has torn this country apart.

We are probably much more angry than that, but I don't want to go into the foreign policy aspects because I am outclassed here. I know that all of you talk about every possible alternative to getting out of Vietnam. We understand that. We know you have considered the seriousness of the aspects to the utmost level and I am not going to try to dwell on that. But I want to relate to you the feeling that many of the men who have returned to this country express because we are probably angriest about all that we were told about Vietnam and about the mystical war against communism.

## The Truth About Vietnam

We found that not only was it a civil war, an effort by a people who had for years been seeking their liberation from any colonial influence whatsoever, but also we found that the Vietnamese whom we had enthusiastically molded after our own image were hard put to take up the fight against the threat we were supposedly saving them from.

We found most people didn't even know the difference between communism and democracy. They only wanted to work in rice paddies without helicopters strafing them and bombs with napalm burning their villages and tearing their country apart. They wanted everything to do with the war, particularly with this foreign presence of the United States of America, to leave them alone in peace, and they practiced the art of survival by siding with whichever military force was present at a particular time, be it Viet Cong, North Vietnamese or American.

We found also that all too often American men were dying in those rice paddies for want of support from their allies. We saw first hand how monies from American taxes were used for a corrupt dictatorial regime. We saw that many people in this country had a one-sided idea of who was kept free by our flag, and blacks provided the highest percentage of casualties. We saw Vietnam ravaged equally by American bombs and search and destroy missions, as well as by Viet Cong terrorism, and yet we listened while this country tried to blame all of the havoc on the Viet Cong.

We rationalized destroying villages in order to save them. We saw America lose her sense of morality as she accepted very coolly a My Lai [site of American atrocities] and refused to give up the image of American soldiers who hand out chocolate bars and chewing gum.

We learned the meaning of free fire zones, shooting anything that moves, and we watched while America placed a cheapness on the lives of orientals.

## The Pitfalls of Pride

We watched the United States falsification of body counts, in fact the glorification of body counts. We listened while month after month we were told the back of the enemy was about to break. We fought using weapons against "oriental human beings." We fought using weapons against those people which I do not believe this country would dream of using were we fighting in the European theater. We watched while men charged up hills because a general said that hill has to be taken, and after losing one platoon or two platoons they marched away to leave the hill for re-occupation by the North Vietnamese. We watched pride allow the most unimportant battles to be blown into extravaganzas, because we couldn't lose, and we couldn't retreat, and because it didn't matter how many American bodies were lost to prove that point, and so there were Hamburger Hills and Khe Sahns and Hill 81s and Fire Base 6s, and so many others.

Now we are told that the men who fought there must watch quietly while American lives are lost so that we can exercise the incredible arrogance of Vietnamizing the Vietnamese.

Each day to facilitate the process by which the United States washes her hands of Vietnam someone has to give up his life so that the United States doesn't have to admit something that the entire world already knows, so that we can't say that we have made a mistake. Someone has to die so that President Nixon won't be, and these are his words, "the first President to lose a war."

We are asking Americans to think about that because how do you ask a man to be the last man to die in Vietnam? How do you ask a man to be the last man to die for a mistake? But we are trying to do that, and we are doing it with thousands of rationalizations, and if you read carefully the President's last speech to the people of this country, you can see that he says, and says clearly, "but the issue, gentlemen, the issue, is communism, and the question is whether or not we will leave that country to the communists or whether or not we will try to give it hope to be a free people." But the point is they are not a free people now under us. They are not a free people, and we cannot fight communism all over the world. I think we should have learned that lesson by now.

But the problem of veterans goes beyond this personal problem, because you think about a poster in this country with a picture of Uncle Sam and the picture says "I want you." And a young man comes out of high school and says, "that is fine, I am going to serve my country," and he goes to Vietnam and he shoots and he kills and he does his job. Or maybe he doesn't kill. Maybe he just goes and he comes back, and when he gets back to this country he finds that he isn't really wanted, because the largest corps of unemployed in the country—it varies depending on who you get it from, the Veterans Administration says 15 percent and various other sources 22 percent—but the largest corps of unemployed in this country are veterans of this war, and of those veterans 33 percent of the unemployed are black. That means one out of every ten of the nation's unemployed is a veteran of Vietnam.

## The VA Hospitals

The hospitals across the country won't, or can't meet their demands. It is not a question of not trying; they haven't got the appropriations. A man recently died after he had a tracheotomy in California, not because of the operation but because there weren't enough personnel to clean the mucus out of his tube and he suffocated to death.

Another young man just died in a New York VA Hospital the other day. A friend of mine was lying in a bed two beds away and tried to help him but he couldn't. He rang a bell and there was nobody there to service that man and so he died of convulsions.

I understand 57 percent of all those entering the VA hospitals talk about suicide. Some 27 percent have tried, and they try because they come back to this country and they have to face what they did in Vietnam, and then they come back and find the indifference of a country that doesn't really care.

## The Greatest Disaster of All Time

Suddenly we are faced with a very sickening situation in this country, because there is no moral indignation and, if there is, it comes from people who are almost exhausted by their past indignations, and I know that many of them are sitting in front of me. The country seems to have lain down and shrugged off something as serious as Laos, just as we calmly shrugged off the loss of 700,000 lives in Pakistan, the so-called greatest disaster of all times.

But we are here as veterans to say we think we are in the midst of the greatest disaster of all times now because they are still dying over there—not just Americans, but Vietnamese— and we are rationalizing leaving that country so that those people can go on killing each other for years to come.

Americans seem to have accepted the idea that the war is winding down, at least for Americans, and they have also allowed the bodies which were once used by a President for statistics to prove that we were winning that war, to be used as evidence against a man who followed orders and who interpreted those orders no differently than hundreds of other men in Vietnam.

We veterans can only look with amazement on the fact that this country has been unable to see there is absolutely no difference between ground troops and a helicopter crew, and yet people have accepted a differentiation fed them by the administration.

No ground troops are in Laos so it is all right to kill Laotians by remote control. But believe me the helicopter crews fill the same body bags and they wreak the same kind of damage on the Vietnamese and Laotian countryside as anybody else, and the President is talking about allowing that to go on for many years to come. One can only ask if we will really be satisfied only when the troops march into Hanoi.

## Congress Must Act

We are asking here in Washington for some action; action from the Congress of the United States of America which has the power to raise and maintain armies, and which by the Constitution also has the power to declare war.

We have come here, not to the President, because we believe that this body can be responsive to the will of the people, and we believe that the will of the people says that we should be out of Vietnam now.

We are here in Washington also to say that the problem of this war is not just a question of war and diplomacy. It is part and parcel of everything that we are trying as human beings to communicate to people in this country—the question of racism, which is rampant in the military, and so many other questions such as the use of weapons; the hypocrisy in our taking umbrage in the Geneva Conventions and using that as justification for a continuation of this war when we are more guilty than any other body of violations of those Geneva Conventions; in the use of free fire zones, harassment interdiction fire, search and destroy missions, the bombings, the torture of prisoners, the killing of prisoners, all accepted policy by many units in South Vietnam. That is what we are trying to say. It is part and parcel of everything.

An American Indian friend of mine who lives in the Indian Nation of Alcatraz put it to me very succinctly. He told me how as a boy on an Indian reservation he had watched television and he used to cheer the cowboys when they came in and shot the Indians, and then suddenly one day he stopped in Vietnam and he said "my God, I am doing to these people the very same thing that was done to my people," and he stopped. And that is what we are trying to say, that we think this thing has to end.

## Crimes and Dishonor

We are also here to ask, and we are here to ask vehemently, where are the leaders of our country? Where is the leadership? We are here to ask where are [Secretary of State Robert S.] McNamara, [Deputy National Security adviser Walt] Rostow, [National Security adviser McGeorge] Bundy, [Assistant Secretary of State Roswell] Gilpatric and so many others? Where are they now that we, the men whom they sent off to war, have returned? These are commanders who have deserted their troops, and there is no more serious crime in the law of war. The Army says they never leave their wounded. The Marines say they never leave even their dead. These men have left all the casualties and retreated behind a pious shield of public rectitude. They have left the real stuff of their reputations bleaching behind them in the sun in this country.

Finally, this administration has done us the ultimate dishonor. They have attempted to disown us and the sacrifices we made for this country. In their blindness and fear they have tried to deny that we are veterans or that we served in Nam. We do not need their testimony. Our own scars and stumps of limbs are witness enough for others and for ourselves.

We wish that a merciful God could wipe away our own memories of that service as easily as this administration has wiped away their memories of us. But all that they have done and all that they can do by this denial is to make more clear than ever our own determination to undertake one last mission—to search out and destroy the last vestige of this barbaric war, to pacify our own hearts, to conquer the hate and the fear that have driven this country these last ten years and more, so when 30 years from now our brothers go down the street without a leg, without an arm, or a face, and small boys ask why, we will be able to say "Vietnam" and not mean a desert, not a filthy obscene memory, but mean instead the place where America finally turned and where soldiers like us helped it in the turning.

# Chapter 2

# Combat

# Chapter Preface

Combat in Vietnam was different from that of any other war in which the United States had fought. The Vietnam War was a guerrilla war, full of ambushes that usually started without warning. A rifle shot, a blast from a machine gun, or a booby-trapped trail was enough to start a mini-battle between the opposing forces. Before the beleaguered troops could figure out where the enemy was hiding or how many there were, the attackers had slipped away into the jungle. Most firefights were short, usually ten minutes or less. Battles that lasted an hour or more remained unforgettable. Any fighting that persisted longer than a day was deemed a "major engagement"; battles that lasted even longer were highly unusual and considered epic.

American troops were not accustomed to guerrilla warfare, and most were not properly trained to fight against an invisible enemy. Most second lieutenants—fresh from their advanced infantry training in the States—lasted only a few months in Vietnam before some mistake killed or severely wounded them (and occasionally members of their platoon) and sent them back home for the duration of the war.

The main duty of combat troops was to go on patrol. A platoon of twenty or so soldiers or Marines would hike out into the jungle day and night in one-hundred-degree temperatures carrying seventy-pound packs. Trying to walk quietly, the troops would search for the enemy, all the while fighting the heat, lack of sleep, poor food, mosquitoes, leeches, sore feet, and their own fear. For some, getting into a firefight with the enemy was almost a relief from the constant anticipation of walking into an ambush or booby trap.

The Vietnam War was more than just a ground war, though. Aviation played an extremely important role. In addition to destroying the enemy, helicopter gunships, fighter planes, and bombers provided crucial support for the troops on the ground. In a typical combat situation, helicopter gunships and fighters would rake the enemy area with machine guns, grenade launchers, napalm, and bombs. The air support was highly successful in permitting American troops to be inserted into or withdrawn from combat areas with minimal casualties to the troops and pilots.

# Every Day Is the Same

Anonymous

For the most part, the fighting in Vietnam was very different than in any other war the United States had fought. The war was mostly guerilla skirmishes with an unseen enemy. Unlike in other wars, the Americans did not start at one end of the country and clear out the Viet Cong and North Vietnamese Army as they worked their way to the other end. Instead, they established base camps throughout South Vietnam. Patrols were sent out from the base camp at regular intervals on search-and-destroy missions to engage the enemy, but these patrols always returned to the base camp and therefore did not hold enemy territory.

The following selection by an unknown Vietnam War veteran in the book *Nam: The Vietnam War in the Words of the Men and Women Who Fought There*, compiled by Mark Baker, describes a typical patrol for his unit. Despite the fear, the days became a mind-numbing routine. The soldiers were always fatigued, not only from hacking their way through the jungle, but from lack of sleep due to night patrols and standing guard. In addition, it was mentally draining to always be prepared for booby traps the Viet Cong had set up all along the patrol routes. The troops knew that whatever happened on one day, the next day would only be more of the same, or worse. It was never better.

Excerpted from *Nam*, by Mark Baker. Copyright © 1981 by Mark Baker. Reprinted by permission of HarperCollins Publishers, Inc.

I t'd get daylight. You get water out of a shell hole and throw your halazone [water purifying] tablets in there so you could brush your teeth. We were pretty ragged, but you sweat yourself clean every day. Then you pull out a piece of C4—plastic explosive—and light it up to heat your food.

## The Patrol

I get out the map. Okay, we've got to go up the blue line, which would be a river. We'd walk down the side of the mountain into the valley. It was harder walking down mountains than walking up.

There were scout snipers with us, so I would use the scope on one of their rifles to check our where we were going. You could see the veins on leaves with those things. I'd send out the flanks for protection of the main body, so we couldn't be ambushed from the sides. It was tough on the flanks, because they had to hack through the bush. The rest of us would be walking down by the river bank, so we had to wait up for the guys out there on either side from time to time.

You'd hump your God damn brains out, up hills, over rocks, through water. Sometimes it was hand over hand through the roots of trees. You sweat your balls off with the sun beating down on your head.

Ninety percent of the time, nothing happened, just boring, a walk in the sun, like sight-seeing. But you're always aware that you could get blown away. You always protect yourself tactically to make sure your ass is covered. Just the dispersion of your people insures that you can put down suppressing fire.

You're hunting the smartest animal there is and that's a human being. You can't believe how fucking smart a man is. If you get one, it's blind luck. In the entire time I was over there, we got one confirmed kill on a day patrol out of battalion. It's their show, you're in their backyard.

## A Simple Life

Hump through the paddies and into the villes. A ville would just be a few bamboo hooches [huts] with dirt floors in a little clearing. Each one had a little shrine inside. There would always be cooking. Their diet was very hot, fish heads and peppers, that type of thing. You never saw any men or even teen-agers, just small children, women and old men.

They pray to their Buddha, go out to work the paddy. Come home, go to sleep. A very simple life. A water buffalo was the family car.

*Exhausted by standing guard, night patrols, and slow progress through the dense jungle, a young soldier rests during a brief moment of quiet.*

"Honcho, hey honcho," the kids come running out of the ville. "Cigmo, you got cigmo, Joe? Chop-chop, you got chop-chop?"

You tell them, *"Didi, didi mao."* Get the fuck away. They'd swear up and down at you. The war had been going on so long there that these kids never had a childhood. You'd be in a fire fight in the middle of a paddy someplace and they would just go right on about their business—a woman and her son with a bucket tied to a rope whipping water over a dike from one paddy to another, old women humping what looked like 150 pounds of brush across their backs.

[General William C.] Westmoreland used to make me crazy with all that bullshit about winning the hearts and minds of the people. Sometimes you felt like trash walking through these villes. Some of the people were beautiful, aristocratic, more civilized than you ever thought of being. They'd come up to you and say, "America and Americans are No. 1 [best]. Vietnam is No. 10 [worst]. You got girl friend? You should be with her. We don't want you here." Who was it that wanted us there?

Sometimes it was beautiful. We were in a bamboo forest and came upon an old Buddhist temple with vines climbing all over it, big Buddhas, brightly colored with reverse swastikas and leaf designs. It felt like being the first explorer to walk into the ruins of Angkor Wat. The monks came out to meet me. I set out some security and made everybody entering the compound take off their weapons. I knew we weren't going to get any trouble from them. They were very educated men, very holy men.

I was constantly fatigued. The killing part is easy but you're just so fucking tired all the fucking time. Your strength is zapped out of your body by the heat. Waiting in a column going down a hill, you go to sleep leaning against a tree. Every day you're out on patrol. Intelligence says they're out there, so here you go walking around in little geometric triangles. Go to this checkpoint, go to that checkpoint, go here, go there. Day in, day out, day in, day out. You get into a mind-numbing routine and before long you're a fucking zombie.

Humans are out there watching you. They know where you're going before you even get there. You see them running very far away in their straw hats and black outfits.

We had a constant attrition from booby traps, seven out of ten casualties a month were traumatic amputees. On a sweep you all get in a long line and walk in. You're watching every place you step wondering who going to hit it. You know someone is going to. Sweep and sweep and sweep, halfway through the day and nothing's happened. Are we going to hit a booby trap today? Who will it be? It was mentally draining.

*Boom!* Just like that and a guy is missing a leg, somebody is missing a foot. Everything stops for a second and there's a lot of action on the radio. A chopper comes down to pick him up. *Zoom*, he's gone. I thought, "Boy, there's going to be a lot of people walking around after this war with no feet." But I still haven't seen them. Where are they?

## Hunting Humans

Then you're back at it again, hunting humans. I hope one shows up, man. I'm going to blow that motherfucker to kingdom come. If the world could only see me now. This is bad news out here and I am bad. We are armed to the teeth. If I could get back to the States with my platoon intact, I could take over the world. Somebody fuck with me, just somebody fuck with me. Come and get me.

When they came to get you—holy shit. I can't even talk on the radio to call in the fire mission. I'm warbling like a kid going through puberty. You swallow slowly and force yourself to say the coordinates. Everything hits slow motion, like you're in your own movie. You try to be cool, calm and collected, and you are . . . kind of. You certainly ain't John Wayne.

Where's it coming from? Who's getting hit? I don't want to die. You can see everything that's happening in immediate terms—life-and-death terms.

## Nothing Like It

When something went right in a fire fight—you call in a fire mission real good, you get your fields of fire right, deploy your men so that you outflank them and you stand up and walk right through them—it's thrilling. There's nothing like it. It's so real. Talk about getting high, this is beyond drugs—ultrareality.

There's nothing like a confirmed kill either. They make you crazy. You want more. You know everybody back at battalion will look at you with envy when you get back in. You scored a touchdown in front of the hometown fans. You get a lot of respect from your peers who are all doing the same thing. When somebody else got one, you'd go, "Son of a bitch, the lucky bastards. Why couldn't we have been there?"

All of a sudden that's over with. It's something everybody talks about to mark the days. A point of reference. You tell the new guys about it. "Hey, remember the day that moth-erfucker, Jay-Jay, jumped up in the middle of that fire fight, man?" Then you go back to the mind-numbing routine. You're a zombie again. Take a walk in the boonies.

It starts getting dark, you occupy the high ground. You set up the perimeter, send out the LPs [long-range patrols]—guys on watch called listening posts. No big deal. I was always near the radio, nothing much happened anyway.

## Night

But then the sun would go down and I could feel my stom-ach sinking. There goes the light. There goes one of your senses, the most important one. Life stops. There's no elec-tricity. There's no technology. It's just hovels made out of corrugated tin and Coke boxes, cardboard, sticks, thatch. There's nothing else over there. The only technology you have is death: M-16s—black plastic rifles—grenades, pocket bombs, Claymores, M-79s, M-60s, mortars, jungle utilities, flak jackets, jungle boots, C4, radios and jet planes to drop the napalm. That was the only technology happening.

You think about people back in the world walking around downtown, going out to get a beer. You'd be staring into the dark so hard, you'd have to reach up and touch your eyes to make sure they were still open.

You try to sleep out there on operations. I'd take off my helmet and my flak jacket and arrange the plates in the jacket just right to fit my back. Then I'd tip my helmet and get my head just right in the webbing. I never went any-where without my lucky green towel. I'd wrap it around my face with just a little hole for my nose. Put on my long sleeve utilities, tuck my hands up under my armpits and just listen to the mosquitoes whine all night long. You know one is going to fly right up your nose and suck the blood out of your brain. It was miserable.

You know it's going to be the same tomorrow as it was today . . . only maybe it might be worse. It won't be any bet-ter. We had a saying about how bad a thing could be: As bad as a day in the Nam.

# Crossing into Cambodia

John B. Morgan

Unlike many other wars the United States has fought, the war in Vietnam was limited by political borders. Official U.S. policy prohibited American soldiers and aircraft from fighting in or pursuing the Viet Cong or North Vietnamese Army into Laos or Cambodia, two countries that bordered Vietnam on the west. The Viet Cong and the NVA took full advantage of this policy by building their supply route to the south, named the Ho Chi Minh Trail, in Laos and Cambodia. The VC also established many command posts in these two countries, crossing over the border to attack the Americans and then returning to safety.

Despite the policy prohibiting U.S. attacks on VC and NVA in Laos and Cambodia, many American soldiers and pilots inadvertently or deliberately strayed across the border. In the following reading, John B. Morgan, who served two tours in Vietnam as a helicopter pilot, tells of an incident during his second tour when he flew a Cobra helicopter (an attack gunship). His team of two surveillance helicopters and two Cobra attack helicopters strayed over the border into Cambodia. When the people on the ground started shooting at the helicopters with rifles, Morgan and the other pilots knew they were taking fire from Viet Cong soldiers since the Cambodians did not have weapons. Soon other American helicopters joined Morgan and his crew, shooting at anything that moved on the ground. When the Americans returned to their base at Pleiku, they were disciplined by their superior officers

Excerpted from "The Wrecking of Old 888," by John B. Morgan, © 1988 John B. Morgan, in *Life on the Line: Stories of Vietnam Air Combat*, edited by Philip D. Chinnery. Reprinted by permission of St. Martin's Press, LLC.

for disregarding the order against fighting in Cambodia. At that point, Morgan knew the United States would never win the war in Vietnam.

Morgan's retelling of his attack on Laos is from *Life on the Line: Stories of Vietnam Air Combat*, by Philip D. Chinnery.

After completing my year in-country [in Vietnam] I was posted to Germany. I was stationed at Ludwigsburg, which is just north of Stuttgart. I had my own little aviation section to provide the 3rd Support Brigade Commander with helicopter support. We had a CH-34C and in eight months I put in 350 hours, which isn't bad for a peacetime unit. However, the challenge soon wore off and I missed the special something that combat flying gave me. When people really need and really appreciate what you can do for them, life takes on a new meaning. It's an elixir which, once tasted, is tough to put down.

## Transfer to Vietnam

In any case I requested transfer to Vietnam. Some of my friends thought I had slipped a gear . . . perhaps I had. I was drinking too much and not at all happy. As it turned out, I may have made a good choice. . . I'm still alive and some of those same friends didn't make it back through their second tours. Shortly after I went back to Vietnam, the Department of the Army started ordering most of my flight school classmates back also. It seems there was a shortage of pilots in the pipeline and my class, as well as the one ahead and one behind, were called upon for a second trip, even though it may have been less than a year to ETS (estimated time in service).

My orders came back with Cobra transition and instructor pilots school en route. It didn't really excite me as they tried to extend my ETS by a year as a 'cost' of the school. I wrote the Pentagon and pointed out that the school was their idea and that I would attend only if my ETS remained August 1969. I got the school and kept the August 1969 ETS.

I would have preferred to drive slicks again, but once you have a talent they use it.

Nha Trang was where I was supposed to go. It was a gravy assignment—villas by the sea, palm trees—but it was not to be. When I arrived at the replacement depot at Bien Hoa they were nice enough to give me a choice: 9th Infantry

*Despite the policy prohibiting U.S. attacks on the Viet Cong and North Vietnamese army in Cambodia, many American soldiers and pilots inadvertently or deliberately strayed across the border.*

Division in the Parrot's Beak or the 4th Infantry at Pleiku. I said 'You can't do this to me. . . I have orders to Nha Trang!' They said, 'If you don't make a choice, we'll assign you.' I had just finished reading an article in the *Stars and Stripes* detailing how the 9th was currently getting its ass kicked, so I reasoned that since I already knew the Central Highlands, and how to best stay alive in that area of operations, I would be better off not jumping into a fire fight in unfamiliar territory. So I was back to the red dust at Pleiku in December 1968, during the dry northwest monsoon. . . .

## Flying Cobras

Flying guns isn't as rewarding as slicks [Huey helicopter, an all-purpose helicopter]. Unless there was a combat assault to cover, we spent a lot of time on standby, either down at the operations shack on the airfield, or at the 2nd Brigade's forward HQ [headquarters], at a place they called 'The Oasis,' about twenty miles west. The aircraft were kept in revetments built of sandbags about chest high. All the time I was there they never suffered any hits from incoming. We worked in pairs—always. Two ships made up a gun team. We had four Cobra teams and four Loaches [small surveillance helicopters] which were used for scouting. The company never did get rid of all the UH-1Cs [Hueys] while I was there. I believe we had two teams of C models up until the time I went home.

One of the Loaches had a people-sniffer device which would sample the air for combustion nuclei, such as camp fires and ammonia, as he flew low-level over a search area. That aircraft would be trailed within gun range by a Cobra. The second snake [Cobra] provided cover for the first and flew at sufficient height so its pilot could direct the people-sniffer using a topographical map. The other Loach stayed up high enough to provide radio relay to base camp in order to get permission to fire on targets.

When the people-sniffer operator got a reading he would transmit 'Mark' or 'Heavy mark.' The directing Cobra pilot would note the location on his map. The sniffer Loach would be directed 'Left five degrees' or 'Right five degrees' to keep him on the grid line. When a search area had been covered thoroughly the heaviest concentrations were compensated for wind drift and permission to fire was requested. There were long-range reconnaissance patrols out there watching trails, so clearance had to be received. With clearance to fire we would roll in with flechette rockets and work over the area. Later an LRRP [long-range reconnaissance platoon] team would assess our work.

## Into Cambodia

On one occasion I was acting as director on one of these missions when we happened to stray off our maps to the west. The area was about midway between Pleiku and Ban Me Thuot in an area of flat, brush-covered terrain. We hadn't found anything in our assigned search area and with ample time, fuel and curiosity I worked us west 'over the fence' into Cambodia. About fifteen miles in we started getting marks. The sniffer surprised a 'mountainyard-looking' individual who, rather than being cool, dove for cover. In the hunting business that's called 'fresh sign.' In a mile or so we got a very hot mark. There was a well-defined trail leading in from the north and out to the south, of what turned out to be a rest area on one of their infiltration routes.

There were numerous hooches [huts] on either side of a stream that made a distinctive meander which was later pointed out to the guys at G-2 [Intelligence]. The more we looked the more we saw, and the sniffer was going off the scale. When the low Loach started taking fire, we had to assume the natives were neither Cambodian nor friendly. They had made a grievous error.

As the Loach pointed out targets we worked them over. There were a lot and they were so confident of our respect of the border they hadn't bothered to dig bunkers. It was a turkey shoot. We went back across the line to rearm and refuel, came back and hit them again. By the time we had expended, word had spread to a gun team from Ban Me Thuot and like sharks in a feeding frenzy they went to work. A

Loach took hits and went down; its crew, however, was rescued by his wing man, but the helicopter had to be destroyed by a team of F-100s [fighter planes] using napalm.

We went back to Pleiku thinking it had been a pretty good day. Not so the General's staff. Our asses looked like hamburger when they finished. To this day I shake my head in disbelief. The handwriting was on the wall.

# A Gunship Door Gunner

Ed Arthur

The Vietnam War saw the birth of many new concepts in warfare. One of them was using helicopters in pairs as a scout and gunship. The scout helicopter was usually a modified troop-carrying Huey or Chinook in which rockets and machine guns had been added. The gunship was an attack Cobra helicopter with rockets, grenade launchers, and machine guns that provided support for the low-flying scout ships. Unfortunately, the low-flying scout helicopters, who frequently had gunners sitting or standing on the helicopters' skids, were excellent targets for enemy soldiers. A crewman on a scout helicopter did not have good odds of surviving his one-year tour in Vietnam.

Ed Arthur was lucky; he survived three dangerous professions in Vietnam: gunship door gunner, "tunnel rat" (a soldier who explored Viet Cong tunnels), and scout crewman in the Ninth Air Cavalry Division. Arthur describes a day in which he was a door gunner for a scout crew in a OH-13 Sioux helicopter. On that day, they found lots of NVA during their mission, and Arthur experienced both fear and exhilaration as he shot at the enemy.

Michael Brennan's book, *Headhunters: Stories from the 1st Squadron, 9th Cavalry in Vietnam, 1965–1967*, includes many stories about soldiers' tours with the Ninth Cavalry, including Arthur's.

Excerpted from "H-13 Scout Gunner, 1967," by Ed Arthur, in *Headhunters: Stories from the First Squadron, Ninth Cavalry, in Vietnam, 1965–1971*, by Matthew Brennan. Copyright © Presidio Press, 1987. Reprinted by permission of Presidio Press.

A couple of days later we were again helping the 3rd Brigade of the 25th Infantry during an operation called Task Force Oregon, barreling in on NVA [North Vietnamese Army] regulars dug in around Duc Pho. By this time the 1st of the 9th was the last Cav unit left that far south. The rest of the division had moved up to take over from the Marines, who'd been getting all the goddamn glory in the papers back home but hadn't been accomplishing doodly shit.

## The Battle Begins

The skipper had the bird [helicopter] about forty feet off the ground when I saw a bunch of [U.S.] dusters (twin 40mm antiaircraft guns mounted on tracks) moving up to enemy bunkers. One tank maneuvered its gun right into the opening of a bunker and fired. The whole damn thing went up, people and all. An arm and a head came up, almost within reach, then fell back, spinning down, head hitting first. Then the dust settled. There was the sharp smell of cordite. I was still seeing the head and arm spinning up, floating down as in the movies, hitting, bouncing up with the dust, hitting once more, all in slow motion. Then, out of the corner of my eye, I saw tracers [bullets] coming at us.

I punched the radio button with my foot and shouted, "Skipper, My God, bank off, bank off! Two o'clock!"

It was a heavy machine gun ringed by sandbags. The skipper saw it too and pulled the bird into a sharp turn to get it out of range. You didn't tangle with a thing like that, but Haselgrove called in its position to get a gunship on it. Word came from Big Six to pull back and help some APCs [armored personnel carriers] get across rice paddies with traps and with trenches dug all through them.

"Here we go," yelled the skipper. "Watch out."

We flew over APCs with guys sitting all over them, as though they were on a hayride or something. We checked out the terrain just ahead and flew back. I was hanging half out of the bird, motioning on the APCs. The young dudes waved at the bird, laughing and shouting, as though it was all a big game. We moved the APCs along carefully while trying to establish radio contact with somebody on the ground to tell those dudes to get off the tops of those vehicles. They were sitting ducks, horsing around, legs dangling over the sides, bouncing along.

## Two NVA Kills

I started to tell the skipper that they must have thought it was a goddamn picnic, but then spotted two NVA in a ditch, raising their weapons. I grabbed the only thing within quick reach, my M79 grenade launcher, which I never could fire worth a damn, swung it toward the gooks, and jerked the trigger, praying that the grenade would at least hit close enough to throw them off. The round exploded before I had time to think about what was happening. It landed right between the NVAs. Shrapnel sliced into the gut of one. The other was thrown up and out of the ditch.

"Go back over," I shouted. I wanted to make sure both gooks were out of action.

Then all hell broke loose. The grenade set off a roar of small arms fire from everywhere. The skipper brought the bird around and made a slow pass over the ditch, only five feet off the ground. I stared at the mess I had made. The one who had gotten it in the gut must have died instantly. He was torn all to hell. The other one could still be alive. I put a single tracer into his forehead and watched the gray stuff and smoke pouring out.

"That got him."

"Boy," said Haselgrove as he jumped the bird about fifteen feet, "you sure did start yourself a battle."

The bird chattered away again while I watched for enemy positions. The skipper made pass after pass, covering the entire area. I dropped smoke grenades to pinpoint NVA bunker positions and entrenchments for the APCs. I was afraid and tight. My leg was jumping again. But more than anything else I was mad, damn good and mad at the gooks holed up down there. I just kept working over the area with Haselgrove, staying on top of the fear.

"I wish I had one of those strip-mining rigs. I'd scoop

those sons of bitches right out of the ground." The skipper laughed at my joke.

## Body Count

Down close to the tree line was a guy standing stiffly up against a tree to stay out of sight. I motioned the skipper to go over, then machine-gunned the gook right across his body with my M16. It was goddamn good to see him flop over. I dropped more Willie Peters [white phosphorous grenades] for the APCs, waving my arm to direct them, then saw another gook crouched in a ditch. I pumped most of a clip at him, blowing the top of his head right off. Next we were over several gooks crawling into a bunker that had bullets pouring out of it. I took a Willie Peter, pulled the pin, leaned far out of the bird, hanging by my left hand with my foot on the skid, and pitched the grenade into the bunker.

"Did you see how many went in there?"

"At least six."

They had to be dead, every last one of them. Smoke was pouring out of the bunker, and of course, there was no more firing from there. The skipper pulled away. I saw another gook running across an open space toward the beach. We were right up against the South China Sea. The gook was probably making for a village along the side of the hill at two o'clock. A Huey gunship followed him, M60 spitting up sand all around his feet. I waited for the NVA to fly apart. I knew what those M60 slugs could do. But the man kept running like mad, arms and legs going faster than I had ever seen anyone run before.

I laughed and punched the radio button. "Hey, Skipper. Look'y there. Bet that guy is clocking better than anybody's ever done at the Olympics."

Haselgrove looked at me, then back at the gook still running with all that machine-gun fire kicking up the sand under him, then back at me again, shaking his head. "Sick joke, Arthur."

I knew it, but pointed, laughing some more, saying to myself, Only don't think, Ed! Don't think, just laugh! "Goddamn if he's not making a world record. If I had my stop-watch . . ."

That's when the whole side of the gook's face went, torn right off, but it wasn't the Huey that got him. He'd cleared the cloud of dust left by the M60, and the gunship had roared over him. I wondered how in the hell they had missed. What got him was the .50-caliber machine gun from one of the APCs. Once again it was like it was in the movies when the film was slowed down. The guy was down in the dust and we were past him. I saw more NVAs cornered in a cane field and fired at them, figuring I probably got several. I was keeping a mental record of all my kills in this battle. After I ran out of ammo, in what little flying time was left, I dropped smoke grenades to help the APCs root out the re-maining NVAs.

## The Battle Is Over

Then, as suddenly as it had started, the battle was over. There were thirty-two NVA bodies, many of them 9th Cav kills, al-though the official score would go to the 25th Infantry. Hasel-grove set down to tell a lieutenant on the ground that he wanted the weapons off the first two gooks I had killed with the grenade. The lieutenant brought over two AK47s [auto-matic rifles] with blood, hair, and skin all over them. The skipper flew them back to Turtle Mountain. I was later given an Air Medal with "V," for valor, because of that battle.

## Shot Down

The skipper and I were shot down two days later. I pulled him out of the bird just before it exploded. The gooks had us surrounded, but our gunships and Blues [Hueys] got us out. I came away with a mouthful of blood, a shattered foot that was bent double up against my leg, and a damaged spine. The skipper had a brain concussion.

I spent two years in and out of hospitals for operations, then managed to fake a physical exam and reenlist. A lot of begging and arguing got me back to the 9th Cav in 1970. I was a jeep machine gunner in D Troop, and we were running rat patrols between Phuoc Vinh and Song Be, down "Ambush Alley." After three months of dodging snipers, land mines, and rocket grenades, my old injuries became so painful that I was put out of Vietnam, and later, out of the Army for good. I was ordered to leave. If my body had held up, I could have done more.

# An Offering to America

Tom Carhart

After graduating from West Point, Tom Carhart volunteered for service in Vietnam, where he led a long-range reconnaissance platoon. In this excerpt from his book *The Offering*, Carhart re-creates the longest day of his service in Vietnam, when his platoon stumbled upon a camp filled with North Vietnamese soldiers. During the fierce firefight that followed, Carhart was forced to confront several unpleasant truths: not all men are brave and war demands that men sacrifice themselves for their country. He describes his emotions when one of his soldiers offered his life in combat.

That night Mad Dog is informed of some changes by Battalion. Our company has to move to its initial point (IP) for descent into the A Shau Valley. I look at the map with Doaks and Mad Dog. We have about sixteen clicks [kilometers] to our IP and three days to make it. It doesn't seem to present any problems. Mad Dog wants to avoid any contact that may slow us down, so he outlines roughly the ridgelines he wants to stay on top of. He casually mentions that he wants my platoon to take point for this movement, and I nod.

## Moving Out

The next day we move eight or nine clicks by about two-thirty in the afternoon and set up camp on the crest of a thickly jungled ridge.

Excerpted from *The Offering*, by Tom Carhart. Copyright © 1987 by Tom Carhart. Reprinted by permission of HarperCollins Publishers, Inc.

The following morning, the third of June, one of the ridges on the map tails off into a swamp, and we find ourselves cautiously edging through brackish knee-deep water and rotting undergrowth. The map shows us high on a ridge, and I am starting to get pissed-off. Mad Dog tells me to move directly west, and within about two clicks it looks as if there is another north-south ridge we can get on that would take us toward our IP. We slog through another hour's worth of swamp. Then suddenly we're mounting a gradual slope.

## Climbing a Hill

We move some four or five hundred meters up this slope, our speed slowing as the grade steepens. Then all the undergrowth disappears, leaving us scrambling up a steep slope dotted with great gray boulders amid the light brown carpet of dead vegetation.

After a few hundred meters we reach a crest. As I climb over the last boulders, the ground suddenly flattens out, and lush green undergrowth is again all around us. I exhale a pleased, relieved breath, then stage-whisper to Sergeant Johnstone, twenty feet away from me and breathing as hard as I was, "Sergeant Johnstone! Hasty perimeter!" I know everybody's going to want to catch his breath as he comes up. I survey the area. We aren't really on a ridge; rather, we seem to have climbed a single steep hill. Off to my left, it looks as if the hill peaks eight or ten meters higher than we are, thirty or forty meters away, but the vegetation is too thick to see that far. I walk back to the edge and look down. I see twenty or thirty men strung out below me, and the tail of that snake disappears into the jungle some two or three hundred meters down the hill. They are moving very slowly.

"Hey, sir, there's a gook shitter over here!" I turn around at this hissed warning from Parker, some thirty meters from the edge of the steep slope, my skin suddenly clammy, and take long strides in his direction. There, another ten meters from the crest, is a small clearing. In the center of this open space four bamboo poles are embedded in the bare dirt to form the corners of a small latrine. A woven palm-frond roof rests on the four bamboo poles. Squarely in the center of this small, protected plot two small mounds rise six or eight inches from the carefully groomed dirt floor, with holes in the center. No question about it, this *is* a gook shitter! I look quickly around like some frightened bird, then stride over to the latrine and get down on my knees, stick my face directly over one of the mounds and inhale strongly through my nose. A strong odor of fish and shit hits my nostrils, and I know instantly that this is an active latrine.

## Under Fire

I stand up and start to turn back when a series of explosions rip the air all around me. I am down on my chest instantly, shaking and scared. Twenty meters away I see the eight or ten men who have made it to the top of the crest scrambling around, shouting at each other or screaming in agony. The fear of God is in my heart now. I look at the top of the hill and see muzzle flashes through the thick vegetation. I hear Sergeant Johnstone screaming, "Up the hill! Get some fire out there!"

I turn and look uphill again. A well-worn footpath leads up the hill from the latrine. Like a zombie, I race up it in a deep crouch, hands sweaty as they grip the rifle stock. I automatically clear the round in the chamber as I run, allowing the heavy metal clunking as the chamber swallows the new bullet to still my heart. Then there is a fork in the path. The path to the left leads directly up the hill, while the path to the right leads around to the right and seems to meander to the top through thicker vegetation. I am only half thinking about anything now, but my heart is leaping inside me.

## Finding the Enemy

I take the trail to the right, bending my body low now as I slow my pace. A sudden noise behind me jerks me around. There, close on my heels, is Specialist Fourth Class Kirby Wilson, a sharpshooter from the Carolina hills. I nod to him, and we began to creep forward again. Off to our left and be hind us we hear the muffled agony of the men huddling just over the crest of the hill. Then two RPDs [enemy machine guns] open up from the top of the hill, in front of us and off to the left. We hear cries and shouts from down the hill now, and it is clear that the men climbing through the cleared area are getting chopped up. Wilson and I keep creeping anxiously forward. I take the heavy white phosphorus grenade off my web gear and straighten the pin so that it can be thrown quickly and easily. As I peer around the edge of a bush, I see two large overhead-cover bunkers some twenty meters away. We are slightly off to one side of them, the firing slits facing toward the company coming up the hill. Behind the nearest bunker three gooks are huddled in animated discussion. I turn and signal Wilson to come up on my left, then ease out from behind the bush on my belly and forearms. Wilson comes into the clear next to me. As we lay there, bringing our weapons up to our shoulders, two more gooks appear with AKs [automatic rifles], then a third. Now there are six gooks in the clearing, four of them quite close together. My weapon is on semiautomatic, and I don't dare switch to automatic, sure they'll hear the click such an adjustment would require. I open fire, watching the enemy's dark shirts soak up my tracers. I get six or seven rounds off before they are able to get out of sight. I have hit only two of them, maybe three.

My adrenaline is really pumping now. I roll onto my left side, pull the pin of my Willie Peter [white phosphorus] grenade with my left hand as I heft it in my right, then heave it up toward the rear of those bunkers with all my strength. No gooks in sight. Wilson throws an M-48 hand grenade and is pulling the pin on another one. I grab one off the side of one of the ammunition pouches on my web belt and pull on the pin. The spoon that arms the grenade is held on with a heavy-gauge cotter pin that normally has to be straightened before it can be pulled. I look down in terror at what can be keeping the pin from coming out, then instantly recall the important cotter-pin-straightening exercise you are supposed to go through before you throw a grenade in combat. I have completely forgotten! I grunt, close my eyes, and strain on the pin. Fear gives me the strength of ten men, and the pin slowly slips out. I roll over again and heave the grenade blindly uphill with all I have. When it leaves my hand, I hear a loud thunk as it hits the heavy branch of a vine and ricochets. Where did it go? A chill of terror is rushing through me when suddenly another RPD opens up, this time spraying dirt all over us as the bullets chew the ground. Wilson and I scramble back behind the clump of bushes.

# Thinking About Death

*Military and political leaders prefer to send young men to war because the young learn and take orders easily and they usually believe, at least for a while, in their own immortality. Philip Caputo, in* A Rumor of War, *has just been confronted with the death of a young enlisted man from his former platoon. The death shocks him and forces him to consider the idea of his own death.*

That suited my mood. I did not feel like talking to anyone. Sullivan was much on my mind, Hugh John Sullivan, dead at the age of twenty-two and before he had had the chance to see his son. Colby had been right; it was bound to happen. But I wondered why it had to happen to a decent young man who always had a joke to tell, and not to some cynical old veteran. I wondered why, it had to happen to a husband and father, and why it had to happen in the way it did. Like many inexperienced soldiers, I suffered from the illusion that there were good ways to die in war. I thought grandly in term of noble sacrifices, of soldiers offering up their bodies for a cause or to save a comrade's life. But there had been nothing sacrificial or ceremonial about Sullivan's death. He had been sniped while filling canteens in a muddy jungle river.

I saw him as Lemmon had described him, lying on his back with the big, bloody hole in his side. I imagined that his face must have looked like the faces of the dead Viet Cong I had seen the month before: mouth opened, lips

There are three sharp consecutive explosions very near us. The last one picks me up off my belly, snaps my head back, and blows my helmet out of sight down the hill. Now that they know where we are, we will do no more good here, and I have to get back to my men.

## Back to the Platoon

We start to scramble back the way we had come, and soon we are back at the juncture of the two trails. Then we race back

---

pursed in a skull-like grin, eyes staring blankly. It was painful to picture Sullivan like that; I had grown so used to seeing his living face. That is when I felt for the first time, sitting in the mess over a greasy tray of greasy food, the slimy, hollow-cold fear that is the fear of death; the image of Sullivan's dead face had suddenly changed into an image of my own. That could be me someday, I thought. I might look like that. If it happened to him, there's no reason it can't happen to me. I did not think it necessarily would happen, but I realized it could. Except in an abstract sense, the chance of being killed had never occurred to me before. As a young, healthy American raised and educated in peacetime, or what passes for peacetime in this century, I had been incapable of imagining myself sick or old, let alone dead. Oh, I had thought about death, but only as an event that would happen far in the future, so far that I had been unable to consider it as a real possibility. Well, it had suddenly become a possibility, and a proximate one for all I knew. That was the thing: I could not possibly know or suspect when it would come. There was only a slight chance of being killed in a headquarters unit, but Sullivan probably had not felt any intimations of mortality when he walked down to that river, a string of canteens jangling in his hand. Then the sniper centered the cross hairs on his telescopic sight, and all that Sullivan had ever been or would ever be, all of his thoughts, memories, and dreams were annihilated in an instant.

Philip Caputo, *A Rumor of War*, 1977.

down the single trail to the latrine and the crumpled knot of my men. No one sees us coming until we are among them.

"Sergeant Johnstone! Get a couple of men over here to cover this trail, right now! Where's Speedy?"

"I don't know where he is, sir. Jaune, Waldorf! Get over by Lieutenant Carhart and cover that trail. Move!"

I look around madly. It looks as if we have twelve or fourteen men on top of the hill, many or most of them hit. I need two warm bodies to cover that trail in case the gooks get smart and use it. "Jaune, get over there, right now!" I look quickly over in Sergeant Johnstone's direction. He is yelling at a man huddled on his side in a fetal position. I quickly crawl-scramble over to him. "What's the matter, Jaune, are you hit?"

"It's my knee, sir, an old basketball injury, I can't move it."

Jesus! A fucking *basketball* injury?"

"Yes, sir, happened in high school, I can't move it." I look into his earnestly pleading face, trembling ever so slightly, terror creeping unwanted up through the cow's lick of milk-white peach fuzz that dusts his throat and jaw. He is frozen with fear, and I suddenly, unreasonably, feel sorry for him. Men are dying all around us, and I need him. But as I look into the cold fright that glazes his eyes, I know that he is absolutely worthless to me this day.

"Fuck! All right, stay where you are. Waldorf, get over there, and cover that trail. Sergeant Johnstone, send somebody else over there with him! Where the fuck is Speedy?"

"He's over here, sir. He's hit; I don't know if he's dead or not."

"Fuck! Sergeant Johnstone, gimme a sitrep. How many men we got up here?"

"Fifteen, sir. The rest of 'em either got back down the hill or else got holed up behind rocks on the hill."

"We got any medics up here?"

"One, sir, but he got hit in the arm. They said Doc Gertsch got caught on the hill, and him and another medic is tryin' to make it up here to us."

"How many Dogwoods [casualties]?"

"One Dogwood six [killed] and seven or eight eights [wounded], sir."

"You hit?"

"No, sir, not yet."

"Okay, how many M-sixties we got?"

"Two, sir, but one of 'em got hit, and it don't work no more."

## Speedy

I crawl over to Speedy's body where it lies slumped in a small clearing on the uphill edge of our hasty perimeter. Wilson crawls with me, having hooked on to me. Speedy is lying on his side with his belly toward us. His eyes are closed, and I can see only two large splotches of blood, one on his right calf, the other on the inside of his left thigh.

The gooks are firing RPG bazooka-type weapons into our positions and even throwing hand grenades downhill the thirty or forty meters that lie between us. We are slowly being chopped to pieces, and I have to get on a radio to get some artillery or maybe even some air support. As I approach Speedy, I grab his shoulder and shake him gently. "Speedy, you're okay now, we're gonna take care of you. Where are you hit?"

He opens his bleary eyes and stares vacantly at me. "My legs, sir, my legs."

I look down at his legs, then pull him over onto his belly. The splotches on his legs are large, but I can't even see any big holes in his pants legs. I am sure the medics will be able to take care of him. Shouts inform me that Doc Gertsch, the senior medic in the company, and another medic have made it to the top of the hill. "Relax, Speedy, you're gonna be okay. Doc Gertsch is on his way over to take care of you." I start to wrestle with his rucksack and try to strip it and the all-important radio from his shoulders. Wilson helps me, and then it breaks free from Speedy's limp body. Inside, I secretly feel good for Speedy. He got hit in the legs, but he is going to be all right. He'll probably even be going home, especially if any bones were broken by the bullets. Lucky guy.

I then begin talking to Mad Dog, who tells me he has sent the first platoon, under Sergeant Harris, around to the left to try to go up the hill from the other side. He has no word from them except that they walked into a real hornets' nest and were stopped, but he doesn't know how far up the hill they got.

## Dead

As I am listening to this, a medic crawls over my legs and, pulling up Speedy's sleeve, starts to insert the needle attached to a bottle of albumin. Thank God, I think, he's gonna be all right now. But even as those thoughts are flashing through my mind, Doc Gertsch crawls over my legs and up next to Speedy. He puts his fingers on his throat and lays his ear on his chest. Then his voice tears me apart and leaves me stunned. "Never mind this one," he says to the medic inserting the albumin needle. "He's already dead; let's get to the next one."

I turn away from the radio in horror, looking blankly at Speedy as the medics crawl away from him. Dead? Speedy? Christ, I was just talking to him; he got hit in the legs; he can't be dead! I lurch over to him, pick up his limp arm, then thrust my hand around his throat, squeezing hard, desperately looking for a pulse. At first I feel nothing; then I sense a faint, irregular twitching deep in his throat. He's alive! "Doc Gertsch, wait, he's alive, I got a pulse, he's alive, come save him!"

Doc Gertsch is beside me in an instant, his hand quickly replacing mine on Speedy's throat. Silence for a few seconds as I wait expectantly, certain that Speedy will live now. "That's just nerves, sir; that ain't his pulse. He's dead. I'm sorry, sir, but we got other people to keep alive."

I nod blindly, then turn back to the radio, numb and shaken. Speedy dead. I can't believe it. . . .

Doc Gertsch is working on men right next to me, and I hear a couple of muffled moans. Then the reinforcements are among us and edging uphill past us, forming a protective umbrella that will allow us to lick our wounds and struggle back down hill. I am confused and stunned, mired in guilt and self-pity and numbness. I roll over onto my back and see that men who were over with Sergeant Gamel are being guided, at a slow crawl, by some of the men who came up with Sergeant Harold. I turn and grab Speedy by his shoulders, then firmly grab the middle of his shirt with my left hand and begin to snake my way along the gentle downgrade. Parker moves silently with us, helping the body along. After a short eternity and sixty or eighty meters, the steep slope blocks the top of the hill and we are in defilade, now protected from the still-active gunfire. Men begin to stand up.

I stop, soaked with sweat, and stretch my back as I stand up. I lean down and slip my right arm under Speedy's left shoulder, then gradually wedge my left arm under his thighs. With a lurch I lean sharply back, heft his dead weight off the ground, and clasp his limp body firmly to my chest. As I do so, his body seems somehow, mysteriously, to break in half at the waist, and his knees are suddenly jammed into his face as his body starts to collapse in my arms. I grasp desperately at his legs, stumbling off-balance and fall heavily forward onto my face and Speedy's uncaring body. I release Speedy's body and turn to my right, trying to pull my feet free. Speedy's body slumps slowly away from me, his shirt riding up over his back. Where the bottom of his rib cage should have been on the left is an ugly red hole. Out of it ooze pink, red, and yellow glistening tubes and entrails. They cascade down indiscriminately, steaming and slowly uncoiling. I stand up again and bend over Speedy reverently. I pull his shirt back down over this unsuspected death wound and again slip my right arm under his back, lower this time. His head lolls back limply on my shoulder. I slip my left arm under his butt and again lurch to my feet, clasping his body to my chest.

I stumble numbly downhill, following the green figure in front of me. The tears that fill my eyes run down and mix with the snot sprayed over my lower face. I felt a hot, fresh trickle running over my chin and down my throat onto my chest, and I realized that the bandage has slipped off my chin and now hangs cold and stiff around my neck like an outlaw's bandanna after the stickup. I feel a hot spot on my belly and my crotch and realize that Speedy is passing his life's blood down the front of my body.

Soon there is no more gunfire behind us, then we move down a steeper stretch, and link up with more filthy, bearded green monsters that drift out of the weeds. No one speaks. I see people gesticulating up in front of me, but I just keep walking, looking neither right nor left, sobbing softly over the dead body of the son of America I carry in my arms. My blood runs over my chin, down my body, mixes with his somewhere on my chest, runs in rivulets down my legs, into and over my squishing boots, and leaves bloody tracks in the Vietnamese jungle floor. We stumble what seems to be ten thousand endless miles, then stop.

I lay Speedy on an open poncho next to other poncho-wrapped bodies, then stand back up, my aching back screaming unheeded. I look down at his slack, openmouthed innocent face. His eyes are closed. Then, before I can say good-bye, the poncho is quickly and neatly folded over his face, and he is gone. I look down unthinking as I move away. After ten or fifteen steps I stop and lean against a tree. I don't know where I am or what is happening. I close my eyes and breathe deeply. Gradually order begins to seep back into my mind.

I open my eyes and stand up straight, lean back and arch my back, blink hard, and take slow, deep breaths. Off to my right some twenty meters I see ten or fifteen wounded men stretched out on their backs. Twenty meters beyond them an LZ [landing zone] is being chopped out of the jungle for a dustoff [helicopter evacuation]. . . .

## The Offering

The dustoff slicks are now hammering in and out, and I see all the wounded have been evacuated; it is time for the dead to be taken out. I walk over to Speedy's body wrapped in a poncho, bend down, and heave him up.

The poncho starts to slip off, and I feel it drag between

my legs as I walk. I wrestle with it, kick at it, and it finally falls clear. I step into the knee-deep swampy area that has been cleared for an LZ and begin to wade unencumbered, holding Speedy close. His calmly sleeping face softly nuzzles my shoulder.

Oh, Speedy, Speedy, Speedy, you son of a bitch, I hardly even know you, but I know you too well. Just a few days ago you stepped in front of me as we neared the crest of that hill, so that you'd get hit by the expected RPD burst instead of me—to give your life that I, your platoon leader, might live. And now you really are dead.

You should never have been carrying my radio, you dumb shit, with that heavy Mexican accent. Why the hell did I let you stay on? I should have gotten somebody else, you'd still be alive. . . .

I hug him to me as I wade. Wise guy. Smart ass. Kid. The tears well up as his blood resoaks my chest and stomach.

I look up at the dustoff slick dropping from the sky in a blur, the rotor wash ballooning my shirt. I lean back and lift Speedy up, my arms aching.

I am just an American soldier lifting the body of a fallen brother-in-arms up into a helicopter. But at another level I am offering him back to America for all of us over here, as evidence of our selfless commitment. This is, finally and undeniably, the Offering of those in my generation of Americans serving in Vietnam: our lives offered for our country. Speedy's offer has been accepted.

More bodies are being loaded into the other side of the hovering helicopter, and I strain to lift Speedy up to the reaching hands. Then, suddenly, his weight is taken from me, and the dustoff rises, leaving me cold and shaken, a shiver stirring my legs. Good-bye, Speedy. Good-bye.

I stare after the dustoff until it disappears.

# Chapter 3

# In the Rear

# Chapter Preface

During the Vietnam War, approximately 90 percent of the American troops in Vietnam acted in support of those who were actually in combat. Whether they admitted it or not, most troops in the rear were glad to be away from the fighting. Occasionally, an infantryman might feel guilty about not doing the job he was trained to do and request to be sent into combat, but many were content in their relative security.

However, no matter where an American was in Vietnam, no place was completely safe from the enemy. There were no "front" or "rear" areas. During this civil war, battles and skirmishes occurred even in supposedly secure areas. Troops arriving in Vietnam for the first time remember, almost without exception, that their civilian airplanes were shot at by enemy Viet Cong as they descended for landing. American military hospitals and airfields in base camps in "the rear" were routinely mortared by the enemy.

However, being stationed in the rear was usually safer than being on the front lines. It also offered more opportunities for relaxing, living a relatively normal military life, and meeting and helping the neighboring Vietnamese villagers. In fact, American military forces were encouraged to go out into the villages and provide medical aid, help the Vietnamese peasants build homes and bridges, and teach school. These efforts were all part of the "hearts and minds" program that was designed to win the allegiance of the Vietnamese to the American way. The theory was that if the United States provided medical, educational, agricultural, and other forms of aid to the Vietnamese peasants, the peasants would then stop supporting the Viet Cong. The program failed mostly because the North Vietnamese were able to overcome the humanitarian programs' progress with an overwhelming military force that crushed the villages.

# R-and-R in Saigon

Philip Caputo

> After troops had served at least six months in Vietnam, they became eligible to take a short break—known as R-and-R (for rest and relaxation or rest and recreation)—from the war. Their break varied in length from a few days to a month, but most lasted about a week. Soldiers could take a military flight to Vung Tau and China Beach in Vietnam; outside of Vietnam they could travel to Hong Kong, Bangkok, Tokyo, Manila, Penang, Taipei, Kuala Lumpur, Singapore, Australia. Some married service members were able to meet their spouses in Hawaii for a short vacation.
>
> After living in the field for so long, many soldiers and Marines were amazed and thrilled at being reminded of every day conveniences, like flush toilets and sleeping in a bed with clean sheets. Philip Caputo's three-day R-and-R in Saigon is typical of how many people felt at being back in the real world again. He delights in being able to sleep without interruption, sightsee and enjoy the beauty of the city, shop, go to a restaurant and be able to choose his dinner from a menu. But like many, the idea of returning to the war brings a sense of deep depression and thoughts of desertion.

In the company mess the next morning, I sat with my numbed hands wrapped around a mug of coffee. I had not slept after the fire-fight. None of us had slept. We had been put on full alert because an enemy battalion was reported to be moving in our direction. We waited, and, waiting, fought off sleep. A sniper teased us now and then, the rain fell in-

Excerpted from *A Rumor of War,* by Philip Caputo. Copyright © 1977 by Philip Caputo. Reprinted by permission of Henry Holt and Company, LLC.

cessantly, but nothing happened. At dawn, we moved back to base camp, except for those who had to stay on the line or go on patrol.

It was still raining while I sat in the mess across from Captain Neal. Outside, a line of marines shuffled past the immersion burners, each dipping his mess kit into the boiling water. I wanted to sleep. I wanted four or five hours of dry, unbroken sleep, but I had to lay communications wire to a new position. That would take most of the day. I also had to inspect the police of my platoon's sector. Neal had found a pile of empty C-ration tins near the schoolhouse, which upset him. He liked to keep a tidy battlefield. So I would have to make sure the men buried the tin cans. I mustn't forget to do that, I thought. It's important to the war effort to pick up our garbage. A voice inside my head told me I was being overly bitter. I was feeling sorry for myself. No one had forced me to join the Marines or to volunteer for a line company. I had asked for it. That was true, but recognizing the truth of it did not solve my immediate problem: I was very tired and wanted to get some sleep.

## R-and-R in Saigon

Neal said he had been looking at my service record and noticed that I had been in Vietnam for nine months without an R-and-R. There was an opening on a flight to Saigon the next morning. Would I like to go to Saigon for three days' R-and-R? Yes, I said without hesitating. Oh yes yes yes.

The green and brown camouflage C-130 landed at Tan Son Nhut airport in the early evening. We rode into Saigon on a bus that had wire screens on its windows, to deflect terrorist grenades. It pulled up in front of the Meyercourt, a hotel reserved for soldiers on R-and-R. The high wall surrounding the hotel was topped with barbed wire, and an MP armed with a shotgun stood by the door in a sand-bagged sentry booth. Out on the balcony of my eighth-floor room, I watched a flare-ship dropping flares over the marshlands south of the city. Shellfire flickered on the horizon, the guns booming rhythmically. So, even in Saigon there was no escape from the war. But the room was clean and cheap. It had a shower and a bed, a real bed with a mattress and clean sheets. I took a hot shower, which felt wonderful, lay down, and slept for fifteen hours.

## Escape

I found escape from the war the next morning. It was in a quiet quarter of the city, where tall trees shaded the streets and I could walk for a long way without seeing soldiers, whores, or bars; just quiet, shady streets and whitewashed villas with red tile roofs. There was a sidewalk café on one of the side streets. I went inside for breakfast. The café was cool and fresh-smelling in the early morning, and the only

## The Tet Photo

*One of the most famous photos of the Vietnam War shows a South Vietnamese general shooting a pistol at the head of a Vietnamese man in civilian clothing whose hands were tied behind his back. Much of the world was horrified by the image of what appeared to be a civilian being brutally executed by the South Vietnamese military on the streets of Saigon. In truth, the captive was a Viet Cong officer who had just killed a South Vietnamese police officer and his entire family. Photographer Eddie Adams, who won a Pulitzer prize for this photo, explains how he managed to take the photo and how he felt about it.*

As we were heading back to the car, we saw the police walking out of a building with this prisoner. His hands were tied and they were walking him down the street. So like any newsman, you photograph him in case he trips and falls or somebody takes a swing at him, until they load him on the wagon and drive off. It was just a routine thing.

We get to the corner of the street. And all of a sudden, out of nowhere, comes General Loan, the national police chief. I was about five feet away from him, and I see him reach for his pistol. I thought he was going to threaten the prisoner.

other customers were two lovely Vietnamese girls wearing orange ao-dais. The waiter handed me a menu. A *menu*. I had a choice of what to eat, something I had not had in months. I ordered juice, café au lait, and hot croissants with jam and butter. After eating, I sat back in the chair and read a collection of Dylan Thomas. The book, a gift from my sister, took me a long way from Vietnam, to the peaceful hills of Wales, to the rocky Welsh coasts where herons flew. I liked "Fern Hill" and "Poem in October," but I could not read "And Death Shall Have No Dominion." I didn't know much about Dylan Thomas's life, but I guessed that he had never been in a war. No one who had seen war could ever doubt that death had dominion.

So as quick as he brought his pistol up, I took a picture. But it turned out he shot him. And the speed of my shutter . . . the bullet hadn't left his head yet. It was just coming out the other end. There was no blood until he was on the ground—whoosh. That's when I turned my back and wouldn't take a picture. There's a limit, certain times you don't take pictures.

I thought absolutely nothing of it. He shot him, so what? Because people die in fuckin' war. And I just happened to be there this time. This is not an unusual occurrence. I could tell you lots of stories—heads being chopped off, all kinds of hairy stuff.

And I didn't find this out until much later, but the prisoner who was killed had himself killed a police major who was one of Loan's best friends, and knifed his entire family. The wife, six kids . . . the whole family. When they captured this guy, I didn't know that. I just happened to be there and took the picture. And all of a sudden I destroy a guy's life. I'm talking about the general, not the Viet Cong—he would have gotten shot if I was there or not. Look, that's what I was there for. And I'd do it again tomorrow. But I don't like destroying people's lives from a picture for the wrong reason.

Eddie Adams, quoted in *To Bear Any Burden: The Vietnam War and Its Aftermath in the Words of Americans and Southeast Asians*, by Al Santoli, 1985.

As I was leaving, an old woman with one arm came up to me begging. She handed me a note which read, "I am fifty years old and lost my left arm in an artillery bombardment. My husband died in a battle with the Viet Cong in 1962. Please give me 20 piasters." I gave her a hundred; she bowed and said, "Cam Ong." Tell her, Dylan, that death has no dominion.

On my second day in Saigon, I met an Indian silk-merchant in one of the city's noisy, enclosed market places, and he asked how I liked Saigon. I said that I liked it very much. It was a beautiful city, a magnificent city when you compared it to the mess in the countryside. "Yes, you are right," he said sadly. "There is something wrong with this country. I think it is the war."

## Dinner

In the evening, I had dinner on the terrace of the Continental Palace Hotel. The Palace was a very old French hotel, where waiters behaved with a politeness that was not fawning and with a dignity that was not haughtiness. I sat at one of the linen-covered tables on the terrace, beside an archway that looked out on the street. A few French plantation owners, old colonials who had stayed on in Indochina, were sitting across from me. Suntanned men dressed in cotton shirts and khaki shorts, they were drinking cold white wine, and eating and gesturing as if they were on the Champs Elysées or the Left Bank. They were enjoying themselves. It occurred to me that it had been a long time since I had seen anyone enjoying himself.

A waiter came up and asked for my order.

"Chateaubriand avec pommes frites, s'il vous plaît."

The waiter, an old Vietnamese man with the bearing of a village elder, winced at my accent. "Pardonneezmoi monsieur. Le chateaubriand est pour deux."

"I know, I want it anyway." I said switching back to English.

"Bien. Vin Rouge?"

"Oui, rouge. A bottle."

"But there is only you."

"I'll drink it. Don't worry."

He wrote on his pad and walked off.

Waiting for the wine, I looked at the Frenchmen talking, gesturing, and laughing at some joke or other, and I began to feel light-headed. It had something to do with the relaxed manner of those men, with their laughter and the sound their forks made against the plates. The wine heightened the sensation. Later, after finishing the chateaubriand and half the bottle of red wine, I realized what the feeling was: normality. I had had two nights of solid sleep, a bath, an excellent dinner, and I felt normal—I mean, I did not feel afraid. For the first time in a very long time, I did not feel afraid. I had been released from that cramped land of death, the front, that land of suffering peasants, worn soldiers, mud, rain, and fear. I felt alive again and in love with life. The Frenchmen across from me were living, not just surviving. And for the time being, I was a part of their world. I had temporarily renewed my citizenship in the human race.

I drank more of the wine, loving the way the sweating bottle looked on the white linen tablecloth. The thought of deserting crossed my mind. It was a deliciously exciting thought. I would stay in Saigon and live life. Of course, I knew it was impossible. Physically, it was impossible. I was white, several inches taller and about seventy pounds heavier than the biggest Vietnamese. The MPs could not miss me. But I was also constrained by the obligation I had toward my platoon. I would be deserting them, my friends. That was the real crime a deserter committed: he ran out on his friends. And perhaps that was why, in spite of everything, we fought as hard as we did. We had no other choice. Desertion was unthinkable. Each of us fought for himself and for the men beside him. The only way out of Vietnam, besides death or wounds, was to fight your way out. We fought to live. But it was pleasant to toy with the idea of desertion, to pretend I had a choice.

Twenty or thirty of us were standing on the tarmac when the C-130 taxied to a stop. Our three days of freedom were over. An old gunnery sergeant stood next to me, entertaining the crowd with jokes. He knew more jokes than a stage comedian, and he told them one after another. He had fought on Iwo Jima and in Korea and had been in Vietnam for seven months. He was a veteran, and with his brown, lined face, he looked it. His rapid-fire jokes kept us laughing, kept us from thinking about where we were going. Perhaps he was trying to keep himself from thinking. But the jokes and laughter stopped when the hatch of the C-130 opened and they brought the bodies off. The corpses were in green rubber body-bags. We knew what they were by the humps the boots made in the bags—and why was that always such a painful sight, the sight of a dead man's boots?

The mood changed. No one spoke. Silently we watched the crewmen carry the dead down the ramp and into an ambulance parked near the aircraft. And I felt it come back again, that old, familiar, cold, cramping fear. The humorous gunnery sergeant, veteran of three wars, shook his head. "Goddamn this war," he said. "Goddamn this war."

# Happiness in a Vietnamese Village

Jonathan Polansky

Many units in Vietnam were stationed in a base camp for extended periods of time. As the Americans got to know their Vietnamese neighbors, they began helping them in different ways. Some brought them medical supplies and treated the sick and injured, while others helped out in orphanages and schools. In the process, many fell in love with the Vietnamese people and their country.

Jonathan Polansky, a rifleman with the 101st Airborne Division, was stationed with his unit to guard a bridge near a small village. During the three months he was there, he met and fell in love with a Vietnamese woman. He and a member from his platoon taught English to the children in the village. For a short time, he was happy in Vietnam. But then his unit had to pull out; when they returned three months later, there was nothing left of the village they had left behind. It had been destroyed by the Viet Cong.

Polansky's account of Lang Co village appears in *Everything We Had: An Oral History of the Vietnam War by Thirty-Three American Soldiers Who Fought It*, by Al Santoli.

The place where we stayed in the lowlands was a little fishing village called Lang Co. A beautiful, beautiful place, on the coast of the Gulf of Tonkin. It was a peaceful little village, a combination of French and Vietnamese architecture, cement buildings and different shades of blue, little concrete houses.

Excerpted from *Everything We Had: An Oral History of the Vietnam War by Thirty-Three American Soldiers Who Fought It*, by Al Santoli. Copyright © 1981 by Albert Santoli and Vietnam Veterans of America. Reprinted by permission of Random House, Inc.

We were stationed on a bridge to protect the village and the railroad from being blown up. That was probably the finest time I spent in 'Nam because I met a lady there who I fell immediately in love with. We'd spend our days together every day. I was pulling night guard duty, so I had nothing to do during the day. We would go across the tracks and lay out by this big waterfall, me just getting into this woman, who had been married to an ARVN [South Vietnamese Army] who had been killed and had a child by him. We would talk for hours and hours. She spoke English pretty well. It was so strange how the conversation would be so close to a conversation that you might have here. We'd be talking about the children and about her and me. How much we enjoyed each other. What we might be doing if we were in the States. What it was like where she grew up in Saigon before she moved up here. She had come all the way up north with her family. Her father was a scholar and was running the school.

## School Teacher

One day a young lieutenant approached me: "Do you want to teach school?" I said, "Yeah, sure." So he said, "Okay, pick out somebody to go into the village with and talk to the hamlet chief." So I grabbed this guy J.J. from Chicago, a big black guy with a big gold tooth in his mouth, bright eyes. We had gotten pretty close. We talked to the village chief and to the assistant of my girl's father. He told us it would be okay, we could work in the classroom with the kids during the day. We couldn't teach them English, but we could certainly work with phonetics, minimal English words and things like that.

The next three months we worked with the kids, teaching English every day. The classes were made up of kids from five years old all the way to teenagers. Me and J.J. would work out little skits to present to the class, like playing baseball with words. We would stand across the room from each other and throw the word back and forth. We'd pronounce it for the kids and they would go along with us. The kids would be roaring, they loved us, to see these two jerky Americans, these two animated young fellas. It was a pleasure beyond belief because each day after class we would go through the village and as we'd walk through we'd hear the little kids whisper to their parents, "Schoolteacher, schoolteacher," and we'd be invited into the houses for soda and tea, and all the kids loved us. They'd come up to us in the street and grab our arm: "Come in here."

After a while I started feeling really, really fine and I

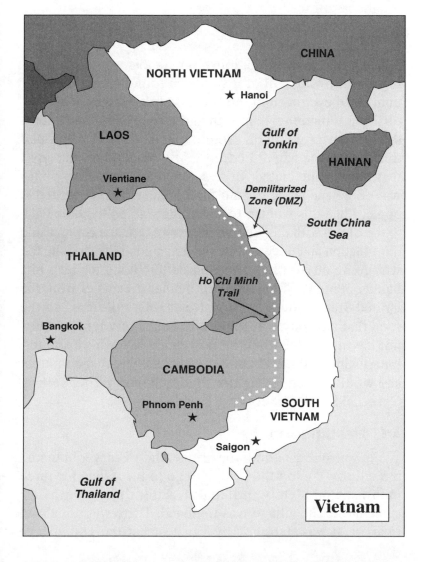

stopped carrying my weapon into the village—which I almost got court-martialed for. All of a sudden I didn't believe the war was going on. I thought I was a Peace Corps worker in this country, dealing with the classroom. I was finding my own little made-up methods to try and relate a little more to the kids. And after the school day was over, I would find myself in the houses with the parents, enjoying talking to them, being invited to the hamlet chief's house for dinner and being catered to. That really brought the roughness off me.

## Dreams

And all this time the relationship with this woman is growing and growing. All of a sudden I found myself happier than I had ever been in the States. I felt like I was accomplishing something. A month ago all the terror and everything that was going on around me, and here I had found this little place where I could really be of some use and I was really appreciated for it. I was really enjoying what I was doing and being treated finer than I was ever treated at home. I had this woman to love. She wanted to come back to the States with me. She wanted to escape the country and the situation and the war. She wanted a good life that she felt was going on over here, compared to having to sleep in a bunker at night. She would tell me her dreams of what the United States would be: big streets, big buildings, all the food that anybody would need to eat, safety for her baby, not having to sleep in a bunker in a place where she felt lonely. She told me about her relatives whom she thought she would never see again. She made her living selling Cokes and whatever else she could get.

## VC Destruction

While we were guarding the bridge, the VC never bothered the village. We left the bridge to go to the Ashau for three months. Completely pulled out. After three months we came back. The village was flattened. There was not a soul in sight. It was flattened by VC destruction. The village was completely burned because all the people were American sympathizers. The only persons left were old bums. The interrogators grabbed them and tried to find out what happened. I couldn't believe it—the village had been so picturesque, the most beautiful little town. Destroyed. Everything was destroyed. Every living thing was gone. I walked into the schoolhouse. I started crying and crying. It couldn't come together for me, after three months in the mountains just thinking about this village. I had totally forgotten about home by that time, after eight months in country . . . after heavy fighting those three months in the Ashau. It just couldn't come together for me.

# Donut Dolly

Jeanne Christie

Not everyone who went to Vietnam served in the military. While there are no official figures, some estimates place between 33,000 and 55,000 American women—military and civilian—in Vietnam between 1962 and 1973. Probably the biggest employers of civilian women were the American Red Cross (ARC), the USO, and the Army Special Services. Jeanne Christie joined the Red Cross's Supplemental Recreational Activity Overseas (SRAO) program that was specifically designed to boost the morale of the troops in the field. During World War II, these women were known as "Donut Dollies;" in Vietnam, they were also called "Chopper Chicks" and "Kool-Aid Kids."

Christie and her peers ran recreation centers in the base camps where troops could play pool, cards, and just relax. She was also sent out everyday in a helicopter to entertain troops in the field—play silly audience-participation games, chat with them, and serve them Kool-Aid. In the following selection, Christie discusses some of the activities she and her coworkers led for the troops she met, the hazards of her job, and the effect it had on her.

Christie's story about being a Donut Dolly in Vietnam is excerpted from *In the Combat Zone: An Oral History of American Women in Vietnam 1965–1975,* by Kathryn Marshall.

After five months at Nha Trang I was sent to Danang, with the First Marine Division. Being with the Marines meant getting out to the field a lot, and doing the job we felt

Excerpted from *In the Combat Zone: An Oral History of American Women in Vietnam, 1966–1975,* by Kathryn Marshall. Copyright © 1987 by Kathryn Marshall. Reprinted with permission of Melanie Jackson Agency, L.L.C.

was so needed. Often we'd fly out to the LZs [landing zones] and at times even end up in one that was hot [under fire]—the situation would change so fast. It all starts to sink in when you're sitting in a chopper and you look back at where you've been and see an air strike going in. The military was careful not to let this happen when you went out in the morning, but as I said, things changed rapidly and counting the bullet holes became a joke.

## A Typical Day

With our work, the driver would pick you up at dawn and you would chopper out to the various units. You'd try to make it to six or eight units before the day was through. You'd talk to the guys and serve them lunch if it happened to be lunchtime, or if you got there early you'd have breakfast with them.

We had some marvelous things happen with the fellows out in the field. One time they brought me chocolate-covered Turtles—where they got them, I don't know. And why they didn't melt from the heat is beyond me. Another time there had been some unexpected changes in the schedule and we ended up sitting on the sandbags, drinking warm orange soda and watching the action in a distant area.

I can recall too easily the first time I really had to go to the bathroom out in the field. For the guys it was easy, but for us it was a different story. I had waited until I thought my eyeballs were going to float before I finally said I wanted some privacy. Out in the field the—quote unquote—privacy might be a bush. But for me, that day, it was some of the fellows holding up green canvas as a barrier. The men said they didn't hear a thing, but I was thinking, "How can I squat and make this quiet?" Then the tinkle tinkle tinkle turned to the roar of an airplane or the rush of a racehorse—the point being that when the men sensed we were embarrassed, they never made an issue of it. They were true gentlemen.

Basically, when we were out in the field the men loved anything we did. For instance, when we went into the LZs the guys would sit on the hill or whatever and watch us in total awe. Some of them would flock to you and talk as fast as they could; others couldn't say a thing. But all of them would stare. They knew every movement we made—nothing we did escaped them.

## Fun and Games

For those who couldn't talk with us, it must have seemed strange to have us drop in from the sky. For the others, it was a chance to laugh and get a bit of relief from the war. Most of the time we took audience-participation programs and Kool-Aid. The audience-participation programs were silly things: question and answer, flashcards, felt-tip pens, rubber bands. All of us had rubber bands, because they were a great ice-breaker. What we did was put a rubber band over a guy's pinky and thumb and tell them they had to get it off without using any part of their body. Eventually they'd start laughing and teasing each other, and before they knew it their minds were on something other than the war.

There were other crazy things we did to divert their attention from the war, but the program was a simple one: the morale of the troops was what was most important. Unfortunately, we were also known as the—quote unquote—fun and games girls, which does not translate well back here in the States. When my children—many years later—asked me what I did in the war, the explanation I ended up with was that some people patched others up, some people shot others, but I played games.

So it was a specific program designed to help the morale of the military we supported. As silly as this may sound, we personified the American women to the men. We were their homes, their sisters, their mothers, their wives, their girlfriends. We were reminders of what they had lost and what they had to continue on for.

I mentioned what gentlemen the fellows could be. Well, they were always looking for ways to help. When I left Nha Trang I was "Jeanne," but in Danang I lost my name tag. Of course, this would put me in an awkward position of being somewhat out of uniform in the Marines' eyes. Anyway, I was down at the flight line center and a gunny [gunnery] sergeant came in with a new name tag for me. It was "Sam." No first name, no last name. Just "Sam."

One morning when I went to work, the Public Affairs Office came in to take shots of us for the public service spots on TV. My blond hair looked great, my smile was perfect, and right on the front of my light blue uniform was my "Sam" name tag. The spots required us to say, "Hi. My name is so-and-so, from the American Red Cross at Freedom Hill." Because I couldn't say my name was Jeanne, with a Sam name tag on, I said, "Sam." It stayed "Sam" after that. I always had fun with it. It made for great conversation out in the field.

## In the Hospital

Programming was sometimes terrific and sometimes the pits. The worst part of working in the Danang area was programming in the morning at the LZs and then ending up in the hospital for the last run of the day. It would just blow your mind to see the guys laughing with you in the morning and blown to bits and in the hospital by afternoon. That tends to be a real demoralizing item when you're the one passing out the smiles.

When we went into the hospitals to program, we were not supposed to get the men too active. Our job was to look them in the eye and convince them that everything was all right. As difficult as that may have been at times, there were moments when the men were the saviors. One fellow—he had lost both his legs and was being med-evacked out—gave me a safety pin for my belt because he would no longer need it, and I would. Because I had had bad legs as a child, I wanted to—but never did—tell him what a fight lay ahead of him. Instead he turned my psyche around and gave me more than just that little pin—more than a million little pins.

Another time I tried to talk to a guy and he started to cough up blood and mucus through his larynx tubes. But I couldn't be terrorized by it and had to go back and face that fellow; I could do more damage by being offended by his limitations than by being understanding. So I talked to him and smiled and said, "It's OK. Don't talk to me. . . . I'll just stay here and talk to you." You learned to smile and cry at the same time, until you finally built up a facade and could literally look at somebody dying and smile like Miss America or whatever we personified to them.

I remember once getting into an area where I obviously should not have been. People started screaming and yelling at me. I think it was a burn ward and new casualties had just come in. I remember smelling something absolutely putrid—the smell of burned human skin is a hard one to forget. I don't know how the staff, doctors and nurses, learned to cope with so many guys in such bad shape.

The casualties of shrapnel always used to make me wonder. Some were in good shape; others weren't. They all looked like somebody had taken a giant pepper grinder to them.

There are other aspects of the experience that had to be dealt with, too. On the healthier side, the guys in the field had their trophies that they shared with us. Both sides collected trophies, and although I only heard about the VC's, I saw some of the ones our guys collected. I had fellows bring me ears to see, and I thought they were apricots. I remember being shown the scalps of the VC, and little peckers in little glass jars. Because it was a way of survival for some of the men, I tried never to let on or pass judgment on them—again, that would have done more damage than just letting it pass by. In that way I tried to protect the men I dealt with. They had become my guys, and like kids collecting frogs or birds' eggs, the guys wouldn't collect trophies forever. So it was all right. . . .

## Vulnerability

Most people don't realize that there were Red Cross gals who died in Nam. With all of us flying around and traveling all over, it's amazing that there weren't more problems. Most of us thought we were invincible. If we had thought about how expendable we were, or dwelled on our vulnerability, we would never have gone to some of the places we went. If we had thought about the whole thing, we probably wouldn't have gone to Nam.

The three that died in our program were in Nam after I was. One died in a jeep accident, one from a mysterious illness, and one was stabbed to death by a GI.

The problem that nobody talked about back then—having it happen to you was a fate worse than death—is being raped. Normally the men were very good, but rape did happen when they would get skunk drunk or stretched to their psychological limit and just go crazy. If a gal happened to be in the wrong place at the wrong time, it could happen.

As a woman in Nam, if you got raped you really had no recourse.

The military was very nasty about it, and naturally it was always the woman's fault. In Nam I knew of some of the options that were offered any gal who found herself in a family way. None of them were pleasant, and none of them left the gal with an ounce of self-respect. Since Nam, I've heard of many more women who had that happen to them, and they only confirmed what I knew then.

We did have guys attempt to break into our quarters. In fact, one night I heard the dog bark and yelled at this guy. I didn't have so much as a popsicle stick, yet I got him to halt and put his hands over his head until the MPs could get there. Situations like that were a total game of bluff.

There were some spooky things, too. At night I would walk out in the driveway and hear something or somebody running off in the brush. It really made you wonder if you were being watched. We also had some ARC gals' photos appear in VC pockets—they'd taken pictures and were either tracing the gals down or watching them. That was spooky!

I'm not sure what the VC were planning to do to those gals. They could just have been using the pictures as propaganda, or they could have actually been trying to pick them off. You know that there were three German nurses that were captured; only one lived to tell about it.

My last duty station was at Phan Rang Air Force Base. By then I was developing a real negative attitude. I just couldn't smile anymore. I loved the Marines, but I had started to speak up, so I wasn't any use to them.

The Air Force was very different from the Marines. The Marines were dirty and in combat a lot. The Air Force was clean and really didn't kill—only their bombs did. In Phan Rang it was clean, and we never saw any casualties. With the Marines, we'd lived under their standards, but with the Air Force we lived in air-conditioned comfort. Phan Rang was real nice, but it was boring beyond my wildest dreams. Even with the Hundred-and-first on the other side of the base and the Aussies in the middle, it was boring. And even after I was promoted to unit director, I still missed Danang.

Basically, Phan Rang was one long party. We did have some program runs, but as UD [unit director], I wanted to let my new girls go out, so I would hold down the center. With the boredom, I took to doing illegal things for excitement. I got a F-100 fighter ride before I left. I had acquired a G-suit, combat boots, black glasses, and helmet—I looked like Rocky the Flying Squirrel! Another time I caught a flight up to Hue and Danang to get a case of toilet paper. As a honcho, I could go out to the flight line and tell them I needed a ride. The fellows would take you almost any place you wanted to go, if they had a flight booked.

It was insane what I could do and get away with: all the little—quote unquote—errands I had to run. At Phan Rang, I learned to drive a car. I learned on an Air Force staff car. I used to get up at the crack of dawn and go with my—quote unquote—teacher, before the roads had even been cleared.

# Short

I was short by then. I both wanted to get out and to go back and protect my Marines; I wanted to be left alone and I wanted to be busy. It was a crazy time. I was getting fat from the lack of exercise and started to take diet pills, which were legal then and very easy to get. The new energy made me want to take more. Diet pills in the day and parties at night did not do a thing for my state of mind.

At Phan Rang we did MEDCAPing [Medical Civil Assistance Program], in conjunction with programming, at the orphanages. In the orphanages I saw kids that were so badly deformed and injured that—with the flies and all the smells that went along with it—my walls just went up. I had to isolate myself in order to save my sanity. A lot of the gals I worked with liked the orphanages, but I went out a couple of times and said, "This is it!" Because I'd seen enough of the maiming, the destruction, and the hurt. So I stayed at the base most of the time, waiting for the dinner hour, waiting to go home, waiting for the time to pass. I just didn't care any more.

When I was finally able to DEROS [Date Eligible for Rotation Overseas], I left for Saigon. [The] Tet [Offensive] had just started, and I ended up getting stuck in Saigon with several other gals. We had a hard time getting around, and food was not easy to obtain. Cokes and doughnuts were our meals. It was the only time as a—quote unquote—donut dolly that I ever saw a doughnut.

By that time I wanted out. The old story of being put in a pine box even began to sound good. Eventually I ran into a colonel I'd known at a previous duty station and convinced him that if I could get back to Cam Ranh, I could hop a flight out. He volunteered to fly me back to Phan Rang, which was close, and I accepted. That evening he flew me out in a small bird-dog spotter plane. I'll always remember the fires around the area; it was an unbelievable sight.

I got to Cam Ranh the next day and was all set to hop a flight out when they discovered that my passport had not been stamped. I had to go back to Saigon, then back to Cam Ranh. Naturally I missed the flight. So I ended up putting on my flight suit and going up to any aircraft on the flight line that was manifested to leave for anyplace. Finally I talked my way onto a flight that was going to Okinawa, and that, unconventional as it was, was how I got out of Nam.

# Chapter 4

# Wounded in Action

# Chapter Preface

Combat medics, navy corpsmen, and military nurses and doctors saved the lives of thousands of American soldiers, sailors, and Marines during the Vietnam War. The military medical facilities used in Vietnam were quite an advance over what was available in previous wars. During the Revolutionary War, a soldier's family or civilians were expected to care for the wounded. During the Civil War, Clara Barton and Dorothea Dix were pioneers in treating injured soldiers in a professional and efficient manner. Nurses and doctors treated soldiers during World War I in field hospitals on the front lines. By the time of World War II, a system of medical evacuation had been developed in which injured soldiers were sent to medical facilities behind the lines. The Korean War saw the first use of helicopters to ferry the wounded to hospitals in the rear, but the medical evacuation "dustoff" was perfected during the Vietnam War.

The combat medic was a crucial factor in keeping the seriously wounded man alive so that he could be placed on board the dustoff. Acting under enemy fire, with a rifle in one hand and a first-aid kit in the other, the medic raced to the wounded to patch them up as best he could. After he had taped gauze and bandages around the wounds, a dustoff was called to take the injured to the base camp hospital for further treatment. If a wounded American soldier could pull through the first hour or two after being injured, chances were good that he would survive. During World War II, approximately one in three soldiers died of their wounds on the battlefield; by the time of the Vietnam War, it had dropped to less than one in five.

With the exception of heavy battles with the enemy that would prevent a dustoff from landing and taking on wounded men, most of the seriously injured were treated by American doctors and nurses within an hour of being wounded. Such prompt response times drastically reduced the number of deaths from war-related injuries. If a wounded soldier could make it to a military hospital, he usually lived. During World War II, the number of casualties who died after reaching a military hospital was 4.5 percent; in Korea, it was 2.5 percent; and in Vietnam, it fell to less than 1 percent.

# Booby Trap

Lewis B. Puller Jr.

Perhaps a soldier's greatest fear in the jungles of Vietnam was being the victim of a booby trap set by the Viet Cong. The VC were experts in concealing booby traps such as pits filled with pungi sticks (bamboo stakes sharpened to a point that would easily shred flesh). Other deadly traps included rigging grenades or land mines to trip wires. When a soldier broke the wire, usually by walking through it, the explosive was set off. Many mines were set to explode two or three feet off the ground, with the intention of literally tearing a man in half.

Lewis B. Puller Jr. was the victim of a VC booby trap. Puller, the son of Lt. Gen. "Chesty" Puller—the most deco- rated Marine in U.S. history, with fifty-three ribbons and medals—followed in his father's footsteps and joined the Marine Corps where he was commissioned as a second lieu- tenant. He went to Vietnam in 1968 but was seriously wounded just a few months after arriving when he stepped on a booby-trapped howitzer shell during a patrol. Both his legs and parts of both hands were blown off in the explo- sion, which Puller describes in the following selection from his autobiography.

Despite multiple operations and more than two years of physical therapy, Puller was never able to walk again. In 1973, he became a lawyer and an activist for military veter- ans. His autobiography, *Fortunate Son*, won the Pulitzer Prize in 1992. Two years later, Puller committed suicide.

Excerpted from *Fortunate Son*, by Lewis B. Puller Jr. Copyright © 1991 by Lewis B. Puller Jr. Reprinted by permission of Grove/Atlantic, Inc.

As soon as our chopper alighted, the men raced to its yawning tailgate and piled aboard. I made certain we all were accounted for before taking a seat beside the door gunner and giving the crew chief the thumbs-up. As we lifted off, I felt the familiar pull in the pit of my stomach caused by our rapid ascent, and when we leveled off, I relaxed my hold on the side of the craft and watched the blur of foliage passing just beneath us. The sky was streaked with the red of the rising sun, and I realized, as I watched its reflection on the glassy surface of the South China Sea, that at least for today the rain was finished. The pilot nosed down in a clearing between the beach and Viem Dong after only a few minutes aloft, and we scrambled down the gangway and fanned out to take up our positions as he reversed his direction and banked up into the sky.

I concentrated as best I could on making certain that the two squads to my left were on line and in position to hook up with the platoon adjacent to them, but in the confusion and noise from the other helicopter around us, control was almost impossible. The skipper's position was to be atop the high bluff to our right, overlooking Viem Dong, where we had camped the night before Barton died. After I had gotten my men on line, my next assignment was to connect with his location. Watson followed closely in my tracks with the radio, but the two nearest men to us were at least twenty meters away on either side and for all intents and purposes out of hearing range. As we maneuvered, I scanned the area to my immediate front, which I had been neglecting in my effort to maintain platoon integrity.

## Sighting the Enemy

Suddenly I saw a squad of green-uniformed North Vietnamese soldiers begin running out of the village and in my direction. They had apparently panicked when the helicopters began landing and were now probing for a way out of the noose we were drawing around them. As they advanced toward me, I was unable to get the attention of the marines near me, and it dawned on me, to my horror, that I was the only obstacle between them and freedom. I raised my rifle to my shoulder and attempted to draw a bead on the lead soldier; but my first bullet was off the mark, and when I pulled the trigger the second time, my rifle jammed. By now the North Vietnamese soldiers had spotted me, and several of them fired wildly in my direction until they abruptly altered their advance and veered off to my left. Standing alone with a malfunctioning weapon and seven enemy soldiers bearing down on me, I was at once seized by a fear that was palpable and all-encompassing. My throat became as dry as parchment, and beads of perspiration popped out on my forehead before coursing down my face. I turned abruptly, with Watson in tow, and ran as fast as I could toward the safety of the bluffs above Viem Dong, where the company headquarters party was to be located.

A narrow trail led up the hill to the headquarters group, and as I approached, it never occurred to me that the thirty meters between my course and the commanders' position had not been secured. I knew only that the firepower advantage of the NVA squad I had just encountered would be neutralized if I could reach the men milling at the crest of the hill. With only a few meters left to cover in my flight, a thunderous boom suddenly rent the air, and I was propelled upward with the acrid smell of cordite in my nostrils.

## Wounded

When I landed a few feet up the trail from the booby-trapped howitzer round that I had detonated, I felt as if I had been airborne forever. Colors and sound became muted, and although there was now a beehive of activity around me, all movement seemed to me to be in slow motion. I thought initially that the loss of my glasses in the explosion accounted for my blurred vision, and I had no idea that the pink mist that engulfed me had been caused by the vaporization of most of my right and left legs. As shock began to numb my body, I could see through a haze of pain that my right thumb and little finger were missing, as was most of my left hand, and I could smell the charred flesh, which extended from

*The Viet Cong, experts in concealing booby traps, ensnared and severely injured many American soldiers.*

my right wrist upward to the elbow. I knew that I had finished serving my time in the hell of Vietnam.

As I drifted in and out of consciousness, I felt elated at the prospect of relinquishing my command and going home to my wife and unborn child. I did not understand why Watson, who was the first man to reach me, kept screaming, "Pray, Lieutenant, for God's sake, pray." I could not see the jagged shards of flesh and bone that had only moments before been my legs, and I did not realize until much later that I had been forever set apart from the rest of humanity.

# Medevac

For the next hour a frantic group of marines awaited the medevac [medical evacuation] chopper that was my only hope of deliverance and worked at keeping me alive. Doc Ellis knelt beside my broken body and with his thumbs kept my life from pouring out into the sand, until a tourniquet fashioned from a web belt was tied around my left stump and a towel was pressed tightly into the hole where my right thigh had joined my torso. My watch and rifle were destroyed by the blast, and my flak jacket was in tatters; but I did manage to turn my undamaged maps and command of the platoon over to Corporal Turner during one of my lucid intervals. I also gave explicit orders to all the marines and corpsmen hovering around me that my wife was not to be told of my injuries until after the baby was born. There was, of course, no possibility of compliance with my command, but the marines ministering to me assured me that my wishes would be honored.

Because we were on a company-size operation, there were six corpsmen in the immediate area around Viem Dong, and each of them carried a supply of blood expanders, which were designed to stabilize blood pressure until whole blood could be administered. As word spread of my injuries, each of the company's corpsmen passed his expanders to Doc Ellis, who used up the last of them while my men slapped at my face, tried to get me to drink water, and held cigarettes to my lips in an attempt to keep me awake. When the chopper finally arrived, I was placed on a stretcher and gently carried to its entrance, where a helmeted crew chief and medevac surgeon helped me aboard. Someone had located my left boot which still contained its bloody foot and that, too, was placed on the stretcher with me.

As the chopper began its race toward the triage of the naval support hospital in Da Nang, I was only moments from death, but I remember thinking clearly before losing consciousness that I was going to make it. I never again saw the third platoon of Golf Company, a remarkable group of young men with whom I had had the most intense male relationships of my life, and I felt guilty for years that I had abandoned them before our work was finished. I was to feel even worse that I was glad to be leaving them and that, in my mind, I had spent my last healthy moments in Vietnam running from the enemy. I came to feel that I had failed to prove myself worthy of my father's name, and broken in spirit as well as body, I was going to have to run a different gauntlet.

## At the Naval Hospital

In the naval support hospital triage in Da Nang, located just down the road from the Seabee compound where I had feasted on frozen strawberries and ice cream only a few days earlier, the remainder of my clothes were cut away, massive transfusions were started directly into my jugular vein, and my severed foot was discarded. On arrival, my blood pressure had failed to register, but once it was restored and I was stabilized, I was wheeled into the operating room, where my left stump was debrided and left open, and the femoral artery, which was all that remained of my right leg, was clamped shut. The procedure was fairly simple because there was so little left to work with. I remember thinking, before I succumbed to the anesthesia, how clean and shiny the tiles in the operating room appeared, how cold the room was, and how worried the eyes all seemed above the green masks of the doctors and nurses who labored over me.

When I regained consciousness, I was in a clean bed with white sheets. An assortment of tubes carried liquids to and from my body, and when I reached up to remove the annoying one affixed to my nose, I found that I could not do so because both my hands were wrapped in bandages the size of boxing gloves. I understood the reason for my bandaged hands because I had seen my right hand with its missing thumb and little finger earlier, and I also knew that my left hand now retained only a thumb and half a forefinger. The word *prehensile* no longer applied to me. I did not yet know or knew only vaguely that I had lost my right leg at the torso and that only a six-inch stump remained of my left thigh. In addition to the damage to my extremities, I had lost massive portions of both buttocks, my scrotum had been split, I had sustained a dislocated shoulder and a ruptured eardrum, and smaller wounds from shell fragments peppered the remainder of my body. Only my face had been spared. It remarkably contained only one small blue line across my nose from a powder burn.

# Platoon Combat Medic

Daniel E. Evans Jr. and Charles W. Sasser

Each platoon that went out on a patrol or ambush was accompanied by a combat medical aide or a navy corpsman. Commonly called "Doc" by the platoon members, the medics were responsible for saving thousands of lives in the field, not only from combat wounds, but also from more mundane tropical illnesses. They treated the soldiers and Marines for diseases such as malaria and various fevers, parasites, sexually transmitted diseases, and they examined the troops' skin daily for fungal infections. But it was during combat that the medics earned the love and respect of their platoon. If a soldier or Marine was injured, he knew he could count on Doc to race to his side and start the initial medical treatment, even while the platoon was still under enemy fire.

Daniel E. Evans Jr. served as a combat medic for a rifle platoon—First Platoon, Company "B," Fourth Battalion, Thirty-ninth Infantry. When he arrived in Vietnam in 1968, he was afraid of blood and petrified that he would not be able to function as a medic while under fire. In the following essay, he describes his first experience as a medic, racing out to help his fellow soldiers who were injured during an ambush. During the intense firefight, his training and desire to help his fallen comrades overcame any fear or hesitation he may have felt while under fire.

Charles W. Sasser is a journalist, a former Green Beret medic, and coauthor of *Doc: Platoon Medic*, from which the following selection is excerpted.

Excerpted from *Doc: Platoon Medic*, by Daniel E. Evans Jr. and Charles W. Sasser (New York: Pocket Books). Copyright © 1998 by Dan Evans and Charles W. Sasser. Reprinted with the permission of the authors.

Maybe it was my guardian angel. Maybe it was blind fool luck. Maybe it was the suppressive fire laid down by Wallace's men. Whichever, I reached the ditch miraculously untouched by the rainfall of enemy fire. Running through the rain drops, as it was called. I dived and rolled, and I was in the water. Came up sputtering.

Sotello's desperate shout: "Doc, you idiot! You'll get yourself killed."

Fetid water waist deep, chest deep in places. Studded with evil-looking black-crusted reeds and grass. Faint pinkish tint to it now, after all the blood. Heads and shoulders and weapons stuck up from the surface as if they'd been planted there. My stomach rolled over like a squirrel in a cage. Stench of cordite, diesel fuel, coppery blood. Fear and death.

## Carnage and Death

Total chaos. Carnage. It awed me. Sickened me. I was the medic trainee who couldn't watch the Vietnam casualty movies at Fort Sam. Giving a hypodermic injection, nauseated me. But this was no longer training or a movie. It was real, and I was stuck square in the middle of it.

Injured, wounded and dying men called for me.

"Doc, help me!"

"Medic!"

"Doc! You'd better take a look at Harvill's leg."

"Doc! Doc, Stevens is bad hurt!"

"Doc! Doc?"

Death. I had seen it neatly encased in body bags back at the morgue I helped build for the 9th Med. I had not seen it like this—waiting to strike in a blinding flash of light or the split-second impact of a bullet screaming into flesh. Death both of terror and of morbid fascination. Death as the star of a living nightmare from which none escaped.

They're gonna die, I thought. These men are gonna die if I can't help them.

"*Medic!*"

I switched into automatic mode, just like that, just like before. A part of me detached itself from the rest. The detached part of me shrugged its shoulders and watched me go to work as in the drills in casualty exercises back at Fort Sam.

## Treatment on the Fly

Seid was still holding Harvill's head out of the water. I fished up his right leg. Ligaments and tendons dangled ragged from the raw hamburger mass of his thigh. The water was bright red around him. He was losing a lot of blood. Artery severed. I ripped the sleeve off my uniform and used it as a tourniquet. Slapped field dressings onto his other wounds. All I could do right now. I moved on.

A geyser of water exploded a foot ahead of me.

Treatment on the fly. Everyone had some type of wound. I soon ran out of bandages. I ripped up my shirt and cut off my trouser legs to use as tourniquets and bandages. I treated the men in the ditch, then crawled out onto the road to make house calls on those too sick to come to me.

I didn't mark the passing of time, but it suddenly came to

*Medics in the field earned the love and respect of injured soldiers by bravely rushing to their side on the battlefield to start emergency medical aid.*

me that the wounded men were no longer fighting. They were crawling out of the water like primordial salamanders. The rescue party's withering fire had driven off the ambushers. Only one sniper remained behind to cover his comrades' withdrawal. He plinked at us to make us keep our heads down.

Fuck him.

## Help Is on the Way

Other rescue parties were also responding, including additional medics. Jim Whitmore, the medic I had relieved at First Platoon, and a grunt named Ron Miller grabbed their aid bags and jumped aboard one of two Jeeps laden with volunteers the battalion commander and the operations officer assembled. The loaded Jeeps recklessly tore up Widow Maker Alley to get to us.

Lieutenant Bob Knapp, the Bravo Company CO, had been in a meeting with the head province chief when he heard the ambush. He dispatched Second and Third Platoons double-timing it down the road from Vinh Kim. A nervous VC security element blew a sixty-pound Chicom claymore [mine] at the leading platoon, but it blew too soon to cause damage. The platoons rushed right through the smoke and kept coming.

I overheard Sergeant Wallace shouting, "Pinpoint that fucking sniper. Waste his ass!"

I looked up and saw Whitmore and Miller ignoring the sniper, as I was. I had already lost my helmet and rifle and used up most of my uniform. Whitmore dropped down next to Teddy Creech and flung open his medical aid bag. "A dust-off is on the way," he shouted to me.

Creech's left leg, still wearing its combat boot, lay discarded in the road next to the mauled Jeep. His other leg was twisted like that of a cloth puppet without joints. Blood and gray ooze gushed from his many wounds.

Whitmore started to move away. "This one's dead," he announced.

Creech's eyes slowly opened in the bloody mask that

was his face. "I ain't dead yet," he croaked. "Give me a shot of morphine."

The bullet hole in Richard Forte's abdomen had sealed itself. His bloated belly told me all the bleeding was internal. There was little I could do for him. His face was the color of old ivory.

"It's all right. I'm okay, Doc," he groaned. "Doc, the others . . . they need you. Go help my buddies, Doc."

Where did the army get such men—thinking of others while they themselves were dying?

## The Medevac Chopper Arrives

When the medevac chopper arrived, it skimmed in low over the trees, dragged its tail, and sat down on the narrow road in an explosion of dust and sniper fire. Dust-off medics leaped out to assist with the evacuation while the crew chief knelt on the roadway with an M16 across his knees.

"Get 'em aboard! Goddammit, load 'em!" the pilot roared above the whumping of the blades and the engine that he kept revved at full rpm, ready to bolt. An AK-47 [automatic rifle] round bored a hole through the chopper's thin skin.

"We're lifting off. We're going!" the pilot threatened.

We medics were feeding torn bodies into the chopper's belly as fast as we could. The bird's floor was slippery with blood. The chopper kicked in even more rpm. Its skids bounced lightly on the road, kissing it, like a racehorse trying to bolt from the starting gate. The pilot was going frantic on us.

"Fuck it! Fuck it! We're outta here!" he bellowed.

"All the wounded aren't aboard," Lieutenant Knapp shouted at the chopper pilot.

"Get out of the way. We're lifting off."

Knapp shouted something to a sergeant named Sinclair. Sinclair leaped onto the side of the helicopter like a fly and thrust the muzzle of his M16 through the open side window and hard against the pilot's flight helmet. Whatever he said to him had the desired effect. The bird remained nested on the road until it was full of mutilated young Americans.

Sotello and Seid and one or two of the less seriously injured men were loaded onto the battalion commander's Jeep for transport to Dong Tam. Third Surgical Hospital was going to be busy.

## Aftermath

Afterward, stunned and emotionally spent, I stood wearily in the middle of the road and stared without seeing the splotches and puddles of thick blood left around the smoldering Jeep. Patrols out sweeping the area had driven off the sniper. I was glad someone had thought to toss Creech's severed leg aboard the chopper. I don't think I could have checked my gorge otherwise.

"What happened to your clothes, soldier?" one of the battalion leaders demanded.

I wore only my boots and the remains of my jungle trousers. I had ripped off the legs for bandages and tourniquets.

"Where's your helmet and weapon, GI?"

I was too spent to answer. I stared at the blood on my hands. Red gloves. I fixated on them. I guessed I was qualified now to wear my Combat Medic Badge. A sinking hard-knot feeling formed in the pit of my stomach. This is only the beginning, the feeling seemed to gloat. You ain't seen it all yet.

As if from a distance at the end of a pipe, I overheard someone explaining to the officer that I was the medic and I had used my clothing in treating WIAs.

Someone nudged me. A gentle voice. "Doc? Doc, here. You can have my shirt."

# The First Day in the Intensive Care Ward

Winnie Smith

Once the combat medics had treated the wounded in the field, the casualties were evacuated in helicopters—called dustoffs—to hospitals in nearby base camps. Most of the injured were being treated by American doctors and nurses within an hour of being wounded. Such prompt response times drastically reduced the number of deaths in the field. During World War II, the percentage of wounded who died from their injuries was 29.3 percent; during the Korean War it was 26.3 percent. In Vietnam, it dropped to 19.0 percent. Casualties in Vietnam received the best medical care in the history of warfare.

Winnie Smith, like all other nurses in Vietnam, volunteered for her tour of duty with dreams of being a combat nurse. She was disappointed to discover, however, that she had been assigned to the medical ward of the Fifty-first Field Hospital in Saigon, treating soldiers who had non-life-threatening injuries and illnesses. One night her life changed forever when the intensive care unit was overwhelmed by incoming casualties and she was asked to step in and help out. Although she was at first overwhelmed by the number and extent of the casualties, she saw that she could make a difference in the lives of the patients, and she soon requested a transfer to an ICU.

Excerpted from *American Daughter Gone to War*, by Winnie Smith. Copyright © 1992 by Winnie Smith. Reprinted with the permission of HarperCollins Publishers, Inc.

I t's strange to be leaving my ward at this time of night, when the main walkway is empty and dimly lit. My stomach tightens at the sight of an ambulance unloading in the triage area, everyone moving swiftly to check wounds. Turning the corner for intensive care, I follow a gurney carrying a head injury. It turns off, pushed through silver swinging doors into the pre-op/post-op area. Twenty more feet, and I swing open a second set of silver doors.

## In the Intensive Care Unit

Bright overhead lights thrust the ward into sharp focus. There must be a hundred IV bottles suspended in the air, and I'm struck by how noisy it is: the hum of continuous suction machines and oxygen tanks hissing, respirators whooshing and someone coughing through his tracheostomy tube, a hopper flushing in the utility room, and cries for help. As many beds as possible have been crammed into the room— four on each side, two rows of four placed back to back down the middle, and two on the far end. Directly in front of me, closest to the nursing station, a Stryker frame for a paralyzed patient occupies one of the spaces. And every bed is filled.

The patient to my right, closest to the doorway, is staring at me. I try to smile but cannot look him in the eye. Both his legs are missing below mid-thigh, the stumps wrapped in bulky layers of Kerlix dressings. Thick tubes drain blood from his chest into a suction machine on the floor. The same machine also receives chest tubes from a patient in the next bed.

A sudden buzz jerks my attention to a corpsman, who has flicked on a machine to suction phlegm from a tracheostomy tube. I don't move, watching until he has finished and rolls the machine to a patient whose head is swathed in gauze.

"Hey, Watson! Hang more blood on the guy in bed twelve. And while you're at it, make sure he's got a blood pressure," comes an order from the other side of the room.

I can't see her, but I recognize Sheila's voice. When she stands, a chest tube bottle full of blood in hand, she sees me frozen by the silver swinging doors.

"What do you want?"

"I was told you need help," I stammer.

## Shock and Fear

"Over there." She waves toward the pre-op/post-op on the other side of the nursing station, not a trace of a dimple in sight.

The Stryker frame soldier is staring at the ceiling with the same empty expression as the one with missing legs. His body is so swollen that his skin is shiny. And he is motionless on the frame, no doubt a quadriplegic.

When he coughs through his trach tube, I look at him in alarm. His stare falls on me briefly, then returns to the ceiling.

Next to his frame, a chest tube bottle is taped to the floor. I alter course to avoid kicking it, then notice a lot more bot-

---

# A New Way of Treating the Wounded

*The duties of nurses in Vietnam went far beyond anything they had ever done back in the United States. In U.S. hospitals, nurses could not even give a patient an aspirin, but in Vietnam they were expected to perform emergency tracheotomies, start IVs, and close wounds after surgery. Not only had their duties changed, but the way the wounded were treated was different than ever before. Dan Freedman and Jacqueline Rhoads, editors of* Nurses in Vietnam: The Forgotten Veterans, *explain some of the changes:*

Rather, Vietnam was a place where thousands lost limbs from land mines, where there was neither front nor rear, and where a combatant rarely saw the enemy he was attempting to shoot.

This different kind of war brought into existence an entirely new way of treating the wounded. High-powered rifle blasts did not produce neat little holes. The shells ricocheted through flesh, ripping organs and tissue along the way. Medevac helicopters were in Korea, but their use was perfected in Vietnam. The Huey dust-off flights may have intles taped to the floor—big bottles for chest drainage, recycled IV bottles for urine, and plasma bottles for bile.

A patient against the far wall is waving at me to come over. I'm scared of him, of this place. I pretend not to see his wave and pass through the empty nursing station.

Four beds line the near wall, and three more loom in the center of the room—all filled. More wounded lie on gurneys with more bottles hung in the air and taped to the floor. But I'm only vaguely aware of these things. My eyes are riveted on the casualty closest to me.

He is part of a body, ragged edges of torn tissues where there once were legs. Part of a body, ripped and torn, bleeding from hundreds of razor-sharp pieces of shrapnel that tore through his face and chest. Part of somebody, dark and mottled from blood and mud and not enough oxygen. Some-

---

advertently compounded the difficulty of treating wounded in a field hospital. The helicopter could swoop down and deliver casualties to the hospital within minutes. As a result, many who would have died in previous wars were kept alive with gauze pads, intravenous connections, and tracheal tubes. Many, however, would not make it. They arrived alive in a technical sense, but dead to the world. Some required neurosurgery too extensive to undertake while other more salvageable cases were pouring through the hospital. Better to save four whose wounds were mendable than one who might tie up the operating room for hours and die anyway, the logic went. This, then, was the basis for triage, or "playing God" as some nurses came to call it.

For women whose careers were built around saving lives, the inability to forestall death was sometimes hard to take. Serious head and chest wounds were put into the "expectant" category, a military euphemism for those left to die. The nurse's mission to save and heal often was no match for mounds of gored and dismembered human flesh and bones.

Dan Freedman and Jacqueline Rhoads, *Nurses in Vietnam: The Forgotten Veterans*, 1987.

body who was a whole person just an hour ago.

It's as if I'm floating and everything is in slow motion. Sounds seem shut out from this place, as though all of time stands still here.

"Are you the nurse they sent to help?" The question comes from far away, takes a long time to reach me.

I nod numbly, looking up at the doctor staring at me from the other side of the bed. A nervous twitch bats his right eye.

I'm not sure I have a voice. "I've never worked in ICU."

"You *can* take a blood pressure?"

## Back to Reality

The snide remark makes me bristle, brings me back. Who does he think he is? I place my stethoscope in my ears and pump up the cuff. There's no blood pressure. I try again, holding down panic. Still nothing. I look up in alarm, shaking my head.

"Aramine drip!" he snaps.

I find the medicine cabinet, but I can't find Aramine. A clinical specialist walks in, asking what I need. All I see is his name tag printed in big block letters. It reads "Hooper."

Hooper says he'll mix the drip for me. I'm grateful because I'm not certain how to do it myself.

The doctor is pumping in two units of blood simultaneously. The more he pumps into the soldier's veins, the more oozes out from all the holes.

Not knowing what else to do, I bend to take another blood pressure. Sixty systolic. Not good, but better than nothing. I say the number.

The doctor nods. "Ambu."

I look at the soldier uncertainly. An ambu bag is used to breathe for someone, but he's already on a respirator attached to a tracheostomy tube. Like everywhere else, blood is pouring from the site.

"Here, pump the blood."

He doesn't sound sarcastic this time, but it would be deserved. What's the matter with me? Am I afraid of a little blood?

He orders four more units of blood from a corpsman, begins squeezing oxygen through the ambu bag.

Specialist Hooper is hanging the Aramine. I watch carefully so I can do it next time. He sets it at a fast drip and leaves to get something for the ICU side.

I stop pumping long enough to get another blood pressure on the patient. Ninety over sixty. When I say the numbers, I feel a rush of hope pass between the doctor and me.

The corpsman comes back with the blood, hangs two of the bottles, and returns to other patients. I stop pumping long enough to replace fluids on a third IV and take another blood pressure. It's still ninety over sixty.

The doctor speeds up the Aramine; I resume pumping. My hands and forearms ache, but I must not slow down. Then, with horror, I notice the soldier's arm is swelling. His IV has slipped out of the vein!

The doctor calls for a cutdown tray. I take another blood pressure. Sixty over forty. I try to keep my voice steady.

The drip is wide open. The faster I pump the blood, the faster it pours out of the soldier.

## Don't Die!

Inside, I'm crying, No! You can't die! This is an American hospital! The ICU! We're here! Please don't die! But I no longer hear a blood pressure. The doctor listens to the bloody chest and hears nothing.

He pumps on the soldier's chest, shouts for the crash cart and bicarb. The corpsman takes over squeezing the ambu bag with one hand, working a blood pump with the other.

My hands tremble as I draw up the 50 cc and plunge it into the IV tubing. "Bicarb given."

"Calcium."

"Calcium given."

The doctor listens to the chest again. He hears nothing. Blood squishes with each compression of the chest. I draw up epinephrine with a cardiac needle, wince as the doctor thrusts it into the soldier's heart.

He listens for a heartbeat. Repeats the procedure. Shakes his head.

The corpsman stops squeezing the ambu bag, clamps off the blood tubing. Don't give up! screams through my head. But I know there is nothing more to do.

Part of me is exhausted beyond feeling. Another part wants to cry. I begin doing what I've been taught to do. I take out the IV needles, despairing of the blood oozing from everywhere no matter how tight the dressings. In time I will know to tie off IV tubes. I remove the silver tube from his throat, cover the gaping hole with a dressing. His eyes won't close. I wrap Kerlix over them.

The corpsman finds me in the utility room, looking for a washbasin. He stares at me in astonishment.

"Forget it, Lieutenant. We're too busy to spend any more time on that guy. They'll hose him down at graves."

The distorted, discolored form is lifted onto a gurney. Dog tags, the ticket for his last ride home, dangle from the dead soldier's neck. He's rolled out the door, and another wounded man is rolled into his place.

# Chapter 5

# Prisoner of War

# Chapter Preface

Americans had been held as prisoners of war in Vietnam from almost the first day hostilities began. Lieutenant (junior grade) Everett Alvarez Jr., a Navy A-4 pilot, was the first prisoner of war taken in North Vietnam on August 5, 1964. Although pilots made up the majority of prisoners of war, soldiers and civilians were also captured. Some were held for years in jungle prisons in the south or in Cambodia. Most of them were eventually marched north to Hanoi, where they spent the final years of the war.

Although North Vietnam had signed the Geneva Convention in 1949, which governed the treatment of prisoners of war, it did not follow the convention's regulations. The North Vietnamese used many loopholes to excuse their treatment of POWs. For example, they claimed that since the United States had never formally declared war against Vietnam, captive Americans were not prisoners of war but "war criminals." According to the Geneva Convention, those who committed "crimes against humanity" were not protected by the humanitarian regulations.

During their time in captivity, most of the POWs were beaten and tortured, shackled or kept in solitary confinement for months or years, denied medical treatment, forbidden from writing or receiving mail, and fed a starvation diet. Some prisoners died from the torture and starvation inflicted on them by their captors. The North Vietnamese used torture in an attempt to get the POWs to "confess" to war crimes committed against the Vietnamese people. Most prisoners, following a set of regulations for prisoners of war known as the Code of Conduct, refused to admit to war crimes until they could no longer bear the torture.

After 1969, when the world had learned of and condemned the torture inflicted on the POWs, treatment improved for most of them. The North Vietnamese stopped the torture. They began to allow the prisoners to receive a monthly letter from home and a package at Christmas. The prisoners were allowed to meet and socialize in a communal area during the day. The quality and quantity of the food also improved.

After the Paris Peace Accords were signed in January 1973, arrangements were made to return the American prisoners of war. Alvarez was in the first group to go home on February 12. The last American POWs were released on March 29, 1973.

# Getting the News

Sybil Stockdale

When an American soldier or pilot became a prisoner of war, his family in the United States suffered right along with him. For many, there was uncertainty of whether their loved one was alive or dead, as the North Vietnamese were not very forthcoming with their lists of prisoners. Families often waited for years to receive a letter from the POW, while the prisoner himself often received only one or two letters a year of the dozens that had been written to him.

Sybil Stockdale remembers what it was like for her and her children after her husband, Commander Jim Stockdale, a navy fighter pilot, was shot down in September 1965. Badly injured during the ejection from his airplane, he spent the next seven and one-half years in a prisoner-of-war camp in Hanoi. She describes how her world changed when she was informed that her husband was missing in action and the elation she felt when she heard that he was still alive. The following selection is from the book they wrote together, *In Love and War: The Story of a Family's Ordeal and Sacrifice During the Vietnam Years*.

On the afternoon of September 9, [1965], I went to San Diego and saw Carol Channing in *Hello, Dolly!* In the darkened theater, waves of nostalgia brought tears to my eyes. It seemed an eternity until Jim would be home in mid-December.

After supper that night, the younger boys asked me to stay upstairs with them until they fell asleep. This old house

Excerpted from *In Love and War: The Story of a Family's Ordeal and Sacrifice During the Vietnam Years*, by Jim Stockdale and Sybil Stockdale. Copyright © 1990 by the United States Naval Institute. Reprinted by permission of Naval Institute Press.

seemed to have a life of its own; it creaked and groaned at the end of the day and frightened young children trying to go to sleep. I remembered my own childhood imaginings about a wolf in the bedroom closet. Even now, more than thirty years later, I hadn't forgotten my terror, so I was more than happy to stay with Stan and Taylor until they went off to sleep.

About an hour later, I realized I had dozed off myself. I listened carefully, thinking I heard voices downstairs. The clock said almost 10:00 p.m. I sat up and listened more carefully. Jimmy was talking to someone in the living room. I headed for the stairs, and met [my neighbor] Doyen Salsig on her way up.

"What are you doing here?" I asked, puzzled. She wrapped her arms around me and hugged me close. "There's been a message," she said, forcing the words out quickly. "Jim is missing." She hugged me even closer.

## Missing in Action

There was absolute silence as I tried to absorb what she'd said. She'd said Jim was missing. Missing! How could he be missing? It was impossible for a person to be missing. You couldn't be missing if you were alive. You'd have to be *somewhere* in the world. God would know where you were.

"Missing?" I said. "How can he be missing?"

"His plane was shot down and they think he got out, but they're not sure. There's a chaplain downstairs telling Jimmy. He has all the details about what they know so far. His name is Parker. He's a lieutenant."

Lieutenant Parker's voice shook as he told me what he knew. Poor young man, I thought as he told me about Jim's parachute having been sighted but no signs of life after the chute hit the ground. This young lieutenant was just doing his job, and I doubted he'd done this before. Several times I asked him to repeat the meager details. There had been no sound from the radio beeper that was supposed to activate automatically when the parachute opened, nor had there been any sign of gathering up the chute after Jim descended.

And that was all they knew. Maybe he was dead and maybe he was alive, so for the time being he'd be listed as missing.

## A Puzzling Sensation

No tears gushed forth. No screams of anguish. Just a puzzling sensation of shock that this was happening to me. Then I began to shake all over. I felt embarrassed to do this in front of Lieutenant Parker, but I couldn't control it. Doyen brought me a glass of sherry, and Lieutenant Parker went over his information once more before he left. He told me to call him if I needed him; otherwise, an officer assigned to help me would call in the morning.

Doyen and I talked about whether I should tell the younger boys now or wait until morning. Jimmy had excused himself and gone to his room while the chaplain was still there. He was trying to be very grown-up and had asked if he could do anything for me. Doyen assured me I should wait until morning to tell the other boys—the words would come once I got started, she said. She asked if I wanted her to stay the night, but I insisted I'd be fine. She made me promise I'd call if I needed her.

After she left, I went to Jimmy's room. He was in bed and music was playing softly on his radio. He asked if I thought Jim was alive or dead. I said I honestly didn't know what to think but that I'd always tell him the truth about his dad. For a long time I sat on the side of his bed and rubbed his back. Then I tiptoed up to my room and got ready for bed. I wondered how to pray, and finally asked God to give Jim and me the strength we would need for whatever lay ahead. Afterward I began to shake again with shock and fear. I remembered all the dire warnings about not talking to the press. I tried to relax but couldn't. I tried to detect whether my intuition told me Jim was dead or alive, but I had absolutely no intuitive feelings about it one way or another. I finally called Doyen and she came back and spent the rest of the night on the sleeping porch.

The next morning I told Sid as best I could and held him in my arms until he'd cried himself out. It was hard to tell how much Stan understood about what was happening. The boys decided it would be best if they went to school as usual; nothing could be accomplished by their staying at home.

Soon after they left, the phone started to ring with official navy messages and friends offering sympathy and support. I still felt only a numb, sleepwalking sensation. The frightening possibility that the news media might descend upon me at any time was an overriding concern in my mind. I felt somewhat reassured by remembering that in the briefing about guidelines if your husband was taken prisoner, the commander had said our government believed the men being held were well treated. If I kept quiet, the navy felt the Communists would continue to treat the men in a humane and civilized way. I felt sure the government had good reason to insist on this "keep quiet" policy.

I did have to establish some sort of premise on which to proceed personally, however. To assume Jim was alive and would return someday made sense to me. It seemed I had three choices really about my personal conduct: I could become an alcoholic and remove myself from reality; I could rant and rave and scream and wring my hands; or I could try to cope as rationally as possible with the uncertainty. The first two choices would only make my life worse instead of better. I needed to be stronger than ever to take care of the boys now, too. I would try to cope and behave the way I believed Jim would want me to. I'd try to make him proud of my behavior if he was alive and if he did come home someday.

## Condolences

During the next few days, food and condolences poured into the house. Of all those expressions of condolence, the one I knew I would never forget came from my own little Stanford. As I was putting some clothes into the washer, he touched my arm and looked straight into my eyes with his big round blue ones so identical to his dad's, and said softly, "Mom, I'm so sorry about dad."

"Thank you, sweetheart," I whispered, and hugged him to me along with the laundry.

## Asking for Answers

I began to read every item about Vietnam in the newspapers and magazines. I reasoned that a war between a country the size of Vietnam and one the size of the United States couldn't last too long. North Vietnam was such a dinky little country, it certainly wouldn't be any match for the United States. I thought it might be a matter of only a few weeks or months before it would all be over.

But even if it didn't last very long, I did need to know whether or not I'd get Jim's pay while he was missing. As promised, people had been assigned to help me work with the navy to find answers to my questions, but I was completely disappointed by the incompetence of the system. I telephoned every day for two weeks to find out whether or not they'd learned if I'd get Jim's pay. The mortgage payment on the house was due the first of October. If I didn't get Jim's pay, I'd have to borrow on his insurance and withdraw money from our mutual fund. It would take time to process the papers to accomplish those things.

I started calling the commander of fiscal affairs at the naval base. He kept reassuring me that he was doing everything he could to find out. Finally, on the last Friday in September, when he still didn't know, I lost my temper and screeched at him: "I've waited long enough! I'll give you until Monday to find out about that pay for me or I'm going to call the admiral in Washington who's head of all navy personnel!"

My temper tantrum paid off: Less than two hours later, I learned I would receive Jim's pay and the check would be mailed directly to me at home. I'd spend it carefully and save as much as I could. If Jim didn't come home, my pension would be only a pittance against what I'd need for the boys and the house. I'd certainly have to get a job, so I'd better save any extra money I could now.

## A New Way of Life

Living through day after day of wondering and never knowing if Jim was alive became a way of life. I asked the navy for an address where I could write to Jim if he was alive. I was told that any letters I sent should be brief and not "too frequent." I decided once a week was the definition of "not too frequent" for me since I'd always written every day or so.

I wrote my first letter on September 26 and my next on October 3, following the addressing instructions the navy had given me: that each letter should be in an unsealed envelope, enclosed in another envelope addressed to Mr. Abba Schwarz, Administrator, Bureau Security and Consular Affairs, Department of State, Washington, D.C. I was told that the State Department would forward my letters through the Red Cross.

Meanwhile, I tired myself out with long bicycle rides, Taylor in the jump seat on the back. I also continued my schedule of tutoring children with reading problems, and began studying everything I could find about the country where Jim might be alive. I found that there were many who believed this war wouldn't be as brief as I hoped, so I changed my expectations to protect myself, and decided I could cope with a five-year span if necessary. I purposely made this time span far longer than I truly believed would be the case, just to protect myself from disappointment.

Doyen was my confidante and constant refuge in the storm. She and Budd were my social companions, too. They'd go with me to watch Jimmy's football games, and we'd often go to the movies at the Village Theater together. They'd include me in all their dinner parties. I would have been lost without them. I was thankful I had to force myself to function normally for the sake of the boys; their needs gave my days a schedule that helped consume the dragging time. I suppressed my feelings as much as possible so as not to frighten the boys. We had found we couldn't talk about their dad among ourselves—it was just too painful. We all went through the routine of each day in as normal a way as possible. I wrote to Jim every week, but never really expected to hear from him.

My birthday and Jim's birthday were long, sad days. I sorted through and removed mementoes from the two gray metal boxes in which the navy had sent home all his personal belongings. On Christmas Day I opened up and wore the lovely blue baroque pearls we'd bought together in Japan. Wherever he was, I felt closer to him with that necklace reminding me of his love. I knew Christmas would be difficult and had made up my mind to try to make the best possible memories for the younger boys. Budd and Doyen and their family came for Christmas dinner. I thanked God that night when the holiday was over. And I wondered what the new year, 1966, would hold for me.

In the days ahead, as I went about my routine of cooking, laundry, mending, helping with homework, I worried about articles in the newspaper referring to the possibility of North Vietnam holding war-crimes trials for the Americans they held prisoner. They claimed our men had bombed civilian targets and so would be treated as war criminals. The dreadful thought of war-crimes trials nagged at me. I took Jimmy into my confidence about it and asked him to try to keep Sid and Stan from being aware of this threat. He was doing everything in his power to be as grown-up and supportive as possible. When the spring flowers began to bloom in Coronado and the North Vietnamese still hadn't conducted any war-crimes trials, I began to feel easier.

## Letters!

On Friday morning, April 15, as I left the house with Taylor to do errands, I gathered the mail from the front-porch box. I flipped through eight or ten pieces, frowning with disgust as they all looked like advertising circulars of one kind or another. I began to take them into the house—then I stopped dead. Wait a minute, the handwriting on one of those envelopes seemed familiar. I went back through the pile and, sure enough, there, looking back at me, was Jim's handwriting.

I picked up the envelope gently, half-afraid it might disappear if I touched it too much. The paper was cheap and there were no stamps on the front but when I turned it over I saw four stamps across the back, all bearing the word *Vietnam*. There was also a round postmark that said "Hanoi,"

My eyes then shifted to the envelope just beneath this one, which also had the stamps and postmark on the back and was addressed to me on the front, but not in Jim's handwriting; instead, the writing was neatly precise and had a European 7 in 547 "A" Avenue.

I stood staring at those envelopes, struck dumb by the magnitude of what I was holding in my hands, and suddenly fearful. Why was the second letter addressed by a stranger? Perhaps it contained bad news. Maybe I shouldn't be alone in the house with a young child when I read them. But where should I go? I knew Doyen wasn't home. I decided to take Taylor and drive to Gala Arnold's. Gala was another dear friend in Coronado. Heading for the car with hands shaking and heart pounding, I thought how I must drive carefully because I was in such a state of turmoil.

When Gala opened her door, I half-whispered that something fantastic had happened. I told her about the letters and asked if I could go into her study and be alone when I read them.

## Important Moment

In the study, I put the two envelopes down in front of me on the desk and carefully examined the handwriting. On one Jim's handwriting looked completely natural. The other was completely foreign. Which one should I open first? This may be one of the biggest moments of your life, Sybil, I thought to myself. It's possible that he may have written one letter himself and later died. The second letter may be telling you he has died.

I decided to open the envelope addressed in the foreign hand first. If it was bad news, I would rather know about it when I read Jim's letter. As I unfolded the cheap manila paper, I found myself staring at a completely unfamiliar handwriting, but the letter began, "My dearest Syb." It was dated 3 February 1966. I quickly skimmed through the four pages and found at the end it was signed "All my love, Jim." So this letter was from him also, despite the strange-looking handwriting and envelope. Now I turned to the other letter and Jim's very familiar handwriting beside the date 26 December 1965. It began, "My Dearest Syb and Boys."

I sat and read these two letters over five or six times each. . . .

## Alive

He was alive. He really was alive. And he sounded fine—just like his natural self. Even some humor, saying the rainy day is here. We always used to wonder if we'd know when the rainy day had arrived as we saved our money in case it did. How incredible to get these letters from him out of the blue. How wonderful to know he truly was alive. How I thanked God for having watched over him.

# Communicating in a POW Camp

Gerald Coffee

From the first American pilot captured in 1964, each prisoner of war in the Hanoi prison known as Heartbreak Hotel was kept in solitary confinement. During the years of enforced seclusion, the Americans were forbidden to communicate among themselves and those who were caught communicating were severely punished. The North Vietnamese knew that permitting communication among the prisoners would improve their morale and help them resist interrogations by their captors. Despite the restrictions and the threat of torture, the Americans devised a communications system that allowed them to talk to each other and pass along news and orders through the POW chain of command.

In the following selection, Gerald Coffee, a navy fighter pilot who was shot down over the Gulf of Tonkin in February 1966, describes how he first learned the secret code that allowed the Americans to keep track of each other during the long years of their captivity. By arranging the letters of the alphabet in a grid and then tapping out the position of the row and column of the letter, the POWs had conversations with their comrades by spelling out every word.

"**M**an in cell number six with the broken arm, listen up! Can you hear me?"

Instantly I was up into a sitting position on my slab; my body tense, the hair on the back of my neck straight out.

Excerpted from *Beyond Survival*, by Gerald Coffee. Copyright © 1990 by Gerald Coffee. Reprinted by permission of Berkley Publishing Group, a division of Penguin Putnam Inc.

Risner! I was sure it was him.

After settling in the night before, I had prayed that there would be other Americans behind those foreboding doors out there. During the morning routine, I had heard some of those doors open and close but they could have been V[ietnamese] prisoners like the ones I'd heard that morning in the huge open compound behind my cell. Even though my hope for contact today had become anticipation, I was still excited by hearing the voice, almost certainly Risner's.

"New man in cell number six, can you hear me? It's safe to talk. We have clearing."

I sprang up to the transom over my door, straddling the space between the slabs and balancing precariously with my good arm. I had already decided the small space beneath the wooden panel covering the barred transom would afford the best view of the dim passageway.

"I hear you, Colonel. I hear you. It's me, Lieutenant Jerry Coffee."

I was startled by the urgency in my own voice. And it was much louder than I had intended it to be.

"Hi, Jerry. Welcome to Heartbreak. Try not to talk so loud. The man in the cell closest to the door is Larry Spencer. He's clearing for us by watching for the guard's shadow as he approaches the entrance. If you hear a single cough or a thump on the wall, it means danger. Stop talking and get away from the door."

The tone of his whisper was dead serious but soft, and I could hear him clearly.

"Colonel, when we talked briefly over in New Guy Village over a month ago I asked if you'd heard anything about Lieutenant JG Bob Hanson, my crewman. Any word yet?"

"No. I've been out at the Zoo for a few weeks and no one out there had his name either. . . ."

"The Zoo?"

He chuckled softly. "That's an old French film studio out in the suburbs of Hanoi. They've made it into a POW camp. There are about forty men out there." Then his whisper went from thoughtful back to urgent.

"Listen, Jerry, you must learn to communicate through the walls. We could be cut off here any moment. You must learn to communicate by tapping on the walls; the system is called tap code. It's the only dependable method we have."

He said "we" and he had said "the man in the cell closest to the door." There are others. Thank God, now I'm with the others. Rabbit had implied there were others, and of course there were the pictures of Alvarez, Shumaker, Stockdale, and Risner I'd seen before. But I was beginning to wonder if I would ever really be in touch with another American.

"How many others are there?" I blurted, ignoring his remarks about tapping on the walls.

"Shhhh! Not so loud! If they catch us communicating like this they'll torture us again just to extract an apology for breaking the stupid prison regulations. Then it can go downhill from there."

"Okay, okay, sorry!" I whispered back, matching Risner's volume as precisely as I could, and truly sorry for having put us at risk. But my curiosity about others persisted.

"How many Americans are here in. . . ."

Thump! Thump!

The "danger" thumps on the side wall reverberated like thunder and were unmistakable in their meaning. They had quickly followed Spencer's single phony cough down near the entrance. I practically catapulted off my tenuous perch, half because I had been startled by the thumps and half because of the adrenaline burst.

A guard entered the passageway and stalked from cell to cell, quietly sliding aside the flaps of rusty tin that covered the little peephole in each door. I was sure I must look guilty as hell sitting there on my slab, my heart pounding loudly. We waited ten minutes.

Finally, a double cough. "Jerry, listen up!" I was back up at the transom instantly.

"Jerry, the tap code is our only dependable link to one another. Somewhere on the walls of your cell you will probably find a little square matrix with twenty-five letters of the alphabet; five rows of five letters each, one row on top of the other. We leave out the letter K because we can use a C for the same sound most of the time."

My mind was scanning back across the letters on the walls of the cells I had been in. Those damn little alphabet things had driven me bonkers trying to figure them out. Now the mystery was about to be over.

The first five letters, A through E, comprised the top row. Then came F through J in the second row, and so on. The rows were numbered top to bottom and the columns were numbered left to right:

|   | 1 | 2 | 3 | 4 | 5 |
|---|---|---|---|---|---|
| 1 | A | B | C | D | E |
| 2 | F | G | H | I | J |
| 3 | L | M | N | O | P |
| 4 | Q | R | S | T | U |
| 5 | V | W | X | Y | Z |

The faceless whisper from across the dim passageway continued. "If you want to communicate the letter A to the man on the other side of the wall, you tap once for the row and once for the column. So A is one and one. If you want a B, tap once for the row and twice for the column. B is one and two. For F, tap twice for the row and once for the column, so F is two and one. N is in the middle of the square, row three and column three, so N is three and three. Z is down in the last corner, row five and column five, so tap five and five. Call up the man next door by tapping shave and a haircut."

He demonstrated on his own door so I could hear it: Tap-tap-tap tap-tap.

"And he'll answer with two bits." Tap-tap.

"Then you go on with your message."

My mind strained to comprehend and retain all I had just heard. Risner continued: "When you are receiving a message, just as soon as you understand the word being transmitted, interrupt with a roger (tap-tap) and the man will go right on to the next word without finishing that one. We use lots of abbreviations for. . . ."

Cough!

Thump! Thump! Thump!

The same guard reentered the cell block. He was suspicious. The afternoon sun was lower now and the entire cell block was in shadow. There would be no more talking today. It became apparent my first communication lesson was over, but I would soon realize that Risner had provided the single most important lesson of my POW life. . . .

I spent hours on the wall with Render Crayton in the adjoining cell. He had been shot down four days after I had, but had made contact with Risner and the others early on. He told me that the report of my shootdown had reached his ship. He recalled reading that our escort had reported seeing my Vigi rolling and tumbling out of control and that it had exploded before hitting the water. Only one parachute had been seen, but no survivors had been determined. Bob and I were listed as missing in action.

## Learning to Use Abbreviations

Render taught me to use abbreviations for our most commonly used words. We used "T" for "the," "F" for "of" "N" for "and" and "in," and "TD," "TN," "TM," "YD," for "today," "tonight," "tomorrow," "yesterday," and so on. I would come to think and speak of the Vietnamese only as the "V."

Almost all commonly used words were abbreviated. The classic was the frequently used word "interrogation," which was reduced to "quiz" and further reduced to "Q." A typical message might be: "This morning I was interrogated by Bug Eye. It was mostly political indoctrination, but he also claimed many American pilots were shot down yesterday." That would be tapped as "TS AM I Q W BUG SOS [same old shit] BT [but] HE SA MANY JOCKS [pilots; jet jockeys) DN YD."

Even at this early stage I was beginning to decipher far more than letters and words from my unseen comrade. From subtle variations in his tapping I could feel urgency, longing, sadness, excitement, and humor. I could tell if he liked my joke, or if it had bombed depending on his extemporaneous scratching, drumming with the fingernails, brushing, or light thumping. What was he doing, laughing or groaning? I was really beginning to know.

We talked about many things those few days of my apprenticeship: our families, our Navy careers, other POWs we knew, how we killed time in prison. Eventually my problem would be not how to kill time, but how to accomplish within each day everything I would set out for myself to do.

## Not Formally Taught

Tap code had never been taught formally in any of our military survival schools. Most of that training had evolved from the Korean experience, and solitary confinement had not been used as extensively by the North Koreans and Red Chinese as it was being used with us here in the prisons of North Vietnam. As it turned out, it is a code as old as prisoners themselves, sometimes even called the "prisoners' code." Fortunately, Air Force Captain Smitty Harris, the sixth American to become a POW here, had recalled it from his stint at the Air Force survival school. It had been mentioned by an instructor almost as an afterthought. When it became apparent that solitary might become the norm, but before the V had actually established it formally, he taught it to the other five men, who all agreed to pass it on to every new POW.

Ideally it would be passed on verbally, as Risner had passed it to me. The next most efficient way was by note, whereby you would draw out the matrix on a piece of paper, writing it with a burnt match stick, a piece of red brick, or (best) with a piece of pencil lead extracted from a pencil left carelessly available in the drawer of an interrogation table. The lead, along with assorted wire, string, nails, and bamboo cuff picks, could be easily concealed in the hem of a shirt or trousers, and thereby usually survive the frequent cell and body inspections.

The code was incredibly versatile, another reason for using it over Morse code. Messages could be transmitted by sweeping, chopping, and raking, using the strokes in lieu of the taps. Almost anything that made sound could be used:

squishing clothes as you wash them, even as a guard was watching, or flapping clothes before hanging them to dry, or pounding on the bottom of your *bo* [latrine bucket] when you emptied it.

## Variations

The most sophisticated variation we called "vocal tap." The normal everyday sounds we make as people were isolated to mean a certain number of taps, one through five. A single cough equalled one tap, two sniffs two taps, a throat cleared three, a hack—as before spitting—four, and a sneeze five. I would have many occasions to communicate my initials, J.C.: "sniff, sniff—sneeze, cough—throat cleared." This was significant, because if I should just disappear from the prison system—and several men would—someone would know when and where I was last accounted for. The roving guards and jailers were always hacking and spitting anyway. They had no idea wc were communicating.

When standing in a courtyard waiting to be interrogated, or later in an exercise yard, I would always know I was being watched by another GI through some tiny crack or peephole in his door or boarded-up window. With my hand nonchalantly at my side I would communicate with him with subtle finger combinations, one through five. This was often the only link between cell blocks and would keep all apprised of what was going on throughout the prison. When the man watching me understood my message he would cough or sniff twice. If he didn't understand or got lost translating, he'd cough or sniff once. Generally two of anything meant yes, go ahead, clear, I understand. One would mean danger, I don't understand, or repeat.

Sometimes a situation would preclude aural or visual use of the code so a note drop would be established. Notes could be written with the usual materials, but if more security was necessary, tiny knots could be tied into a piece of thread drawn from clothing. The knots would be along the thread in number combinations one through five and could be read visually or by feel like Braille; it was especially helpful for men isolated in dark cells, as Risner would be. A piece of wire was sharpened by scraping it on the coarse iron surface of the ankle manacles and then used like a needle to prick tiny holes in a piece of paper in number combinations. The paper could be wadded up and tossed into a corner and if inspected by a suspicious V would appear to be blank. But the GI who knew better would hold it up to the sky or light so the holes would be revealed and easily read: "FNG N DI SA UCLA BT OSU N RB SH." Translation: "A new guy in the Desert Inn says UCLA beat Ohio State in the Rose Bowl. Shit hot!" (FNG—Fucking New Guy—is the derisive term referring to a new man in a military unit or squadron; part of his "initiation.")

## A Signature Sneeze

Actually, the most common form of generic communication I had already learned before my session with Risner. Nearly every man would ultimately develop his own unique signature sneeze. A normal sneeze would be turned to an expletive such as "Bullshit!", "Horse shit!", "Rat shit!" (my favorite), or "Fuck Ho!" meaning, of course, Ho Chi Minh. A man could gin up a good healthy sneeze and practically shout out his pent-up anger, contempt, and frustration. The guards never seemed to regard this practice for what it really was—insults really—and it would afford us some small pleasure in putting something over on them on a continuing basis. Strangely enough, it would become comforting to hear these expletives throughout the day and night; sort of a humorous little reminder that the family was all there, and things were normal; dismal as ever, but normal.

# Torture

Ray Vohden

> Ray Vohden was the fourth American prisoner of war captured by the North Vietnamese. He was the most senior ranking American POW in the "Cuba Program," the year-long interrogation and torture of twenty POWs by agents of Fidel Castro's government beginning in July 1967.
>
> The Americans nicknamed the lead Cuban interrogator "Fidel." When Fidel's genial attempts to get "confessions" of war crimes committed by the American military against the Vietnamese were rebuffed, Fidel resorted to other means to obtain the information he wanted. The POWs were often subjected to beatings and torture that would sometimes go on for days until the prisoners, worn out and unable to take the pain any longer, capitulated to their captors' demands. In the following reading, Vohden describes the interrogation and torture he suffered under Fidel's direction until he finally broke and no longer cared whether he lived or died. Although Vohden and the other POWs broke under torture, he is pleased that none of the Americans in the Cuba Program were brainwashed to accept North Vietnamese propaganda and hence, none were released in the North's early release program.

In August 1964, I was assigned to Attack Squadron 216 as the Operations Officer flying in the A4C Skyhawk off the USS *Hancock*. Our carrier was in the South China Sea in early 1965 when the war against North Vietnam began to escalate. On my fifth mission, I was shot down bombing a bridge in North Vietnam. I broke both bones above the ankle when I

Excerpted from Ray Vohden's testimony before the U.S. House of Representatives Committee on International Relations, November 4, 1999.

landed. I was then taken to the camp known as the "Hanoi Hilton" where I was in complete solitary and was never moved off a wooden board for fourth months, except to go to the hospital for two hours one night to have a two-inch piece of bone cut from my leg because it had become infected.

For the next two-and-a-half years, I was moved from camp to camp until being sent to "the Zoo" in November 1965. Throughout this two-and-a-half-year period, I survived like the other POWs. I lived in a small room, by myself or with one or two men. I was tortured, forced, and/or punished before I wrote my biography and my confession.

## Meeting Fidel

In the early part of September 1967, I was taken to an interrogation [Quiz]. To my astonishment, the man sitting across from me was a Caucasian. One of the Vietnamese camp officers sat next to him. We talked about the war for the next half hour. He had an excellent command of English and appeared to be very knowledgeable about the U.S. and the war. Without question, his presence was almost earth-shaking.

Several days later, I was moved to another room with Jack Bomar and another Air Force officer. They had both recently been shot down and had also talked to the Caucasian. One of us named him Fidel because we guessed he might be Cuban.

Individually, we met with him daily. The war was essentially the main topic. After several days, I concluded that I wanted no part of whatever he was up to. I decided to refuse cigarettes and be as unfriendly and as obnoxious as I could, in hopes that he would consider me unworthy for any purpose he might have for me. He told me he didn't like my unfriendly attitude and that I would be sorry.

I was taken to Quiz early in the morning. The Elf, one of the other Vietnamese officers was there. The Elf asked me what orders did I give when I was in the Pool Hall. I told him none. He asked four or five more times. I said none. He left and came back with 6 or 7 guards. They forced me to get on the floor. They put manacles on my wrists behind me and strapped my elbows together behind me. And for some undeterminable time, I suffered in the straps until he gave me a clue about what the order was. It was about throwing food away. I told him I gave the order.

Five minutes later, as they are taking the manacles and straps off, the door bursts open. In comes Fidel, ranting and raving like a madman, pointing his finger at me and telling me that I better have a good attitude now and do everything he says. I told him yes. He said, "When I give you a cigarette and you don't smoke it, I will make you eat cigarettes until they come out of your ears." Then, he slapped me ten or fifteen times telling me I better do everything he says. I then had to write on a piece of notebook paper that I surrendered to the Vietnamese people and would do everything they want me to do. He told me other things to write and then told me to sign it. Now he says; "Prove you will do everything I tell you to, eat the whole piece of paper." It was hard to chew and did not break up very well, but I managed to swallow it after almost gagging and throwing up.

My shoulders and arms were still very painful but I was still able to use my crutches. I went back to the room I had come from, but Bomar and Duart were gone. They put me in leg irons and cuffs. For the next two weeks, I was beaten three of four times a day until I became demoralized and depressed and started to lose my appetite. I finally gave up eating anything. The last time the guard picked up the full dishes and left, Fidel came in five minutes later carrying the food. He was yelling and screaming at me that I was trying to cheat him again and that if I did not eat, they would hold me down and stuff the food down my throat. I tried to eat but just could not. He screamed at me that he would kill me if I didn't eat. I had reached bottom. Tears streamed from my eyes. I didn't care if I lived or died. Fidel just stood there and watched. Without a word he left. Later that day, I moved to another room. There were no more leg irons, cuffs or beatings.

## New Tactics

A week later, the tactic shifted. Fidel had my meal brought to the interrogation room. He was playing some good Montovani music. He was friendlier now. Bomar, Duart and I eventually moved back together again. All had surrendered. The treatment improved. We got a few extra cigarettes each day. He now brought us tea in the morning and he brought us a chess set. He brought me a cigar to smoke. We told him we didn't want these things. Fidel responded that if we didn't use what he gave us, we would be very sorry. As time passed, we had to carve wooden spoons, toy trucks and cars. One by one, more POWs joined us. All had been forced to surrender. We finally moved to a larger room when the number came to eight. We were able to go outside more often, dig a fishpond and made a fireplace.

At Quiz, Fidel talked about the war and about going home. He showed us pictures of fashion models in magazines. He talked about our wives and our families. We saw articles from *Time* and *Newsweek* magazine, especially anything that was anti war. He tried every argument in the book to convince us that the U.S. was wrong in its war of aggression. Every day, he reminded us not to become reactionary or we would suffer; that what he had given us before was just a sample of what would come.

On a weekly basis, he would give us the opportunity to give our true feeling on the war. I always told him the same. I told him that the U.S. was right in the war and that I supported our President.

## Torture

This new nicer strategy did not last long. It was intermittently combined with torture.

One morning in early March 1968, one of the camp officers came to the outside of our room and disconnected the wires to our speaker. This gave rise to all kinds of speculation. Later that day, we heard from the guys in another building who had heard the radio program, that the first three U.S. prisoners had been released by the Vietnamese. The rest of the camp heard the radio that morning and the news of the release, I felt very relieved and proud of myself and the others who served with me in the Fidel program because, although I can't say for sure what the original purpose of Fidel's presence was, I believe the way the program was run, that its purpose was to find someone who could be of value to the North Vietnamese if released. It was evident that they wanted to release some prisoners because they did.

Some found it hard to believe that Fidel expected us to adopt the enemy views on the war and talk about good treatment after we were tortured and forced to surrender. But, after getting to know Fidel, I could see how this was his goal and how he believed that he could make this happen.

After Fidel failed in having any of his group released, his program continued without any real purpose or meaning.

# Chapter 6

# The Enemy

# Chapter Preface

For Americans fighting in Vietnam, determining who was the enemy was a huge problem, and one that was not readily resolved. Since the war was essentially a civil war between the Communist-led Viet Cong and North Vietnamese and the American-supported South Vietnamese, it was almost impossible to know who supported the Communists and who did not. During the day, Vietnamese villagers were frequently peaceful and friendly toward American soldiers and often worked as merchants, maids, or barbers for them in their base camps. But at night, these same villagers became the enemy who slipped through fences to blow up the military compounds. Many Americans have reported their dismay at discovering that their favorite maid or shoeshine boy was shot trying to infiltrate the base's perimeter during an attack by the VC at night.

The Americans were also unsure about the Vietnamese because many children were recruited by the Viet Cong. The VC began indoctrinating children in the war against Americans almost from infancy. Children were taught that they were needed to liberate Vietnam from the capitalist-colonial empires of first France and then the United States. To achieve this, they were taught the art of deception. The Viet Cong emphasized that telling lies was just as effective in defeating their enemies as killing them.

The children were also very impressionable and from early on believed that sacrificing their lives in the war against the Americans was a courageous act. Children were taught to throw grenades into bars, restaurants, marketplaces, and other areas frequented by Americans. The Vietnamese also used infants to kill Americans. Many Vietnam veterans have related stories about members of their units who were killed when they picked up a crying Vietnamese baby who had been booby-trapped with a grenade. Using children to kill was a form of psychological warfare; after Americans had witnessed several instances of their fellow soldiers being killed by Vietnamese children, they began to suspect all Vietnamese as being the enemy. Their suspicions would turn to hate; Americans then found it difficult to make friends with villagers whom they believed were trying to kill them. In addition, when threatened by children, American soldiers would feel ashamed and guilty for shooting or killing them. This psychological warfare was one of the Viet Cong's most successful weapons against the Americans during the war.

# Why We Must Fight

Le Ly Hayslip

Many Americans did not understand why the Vietnamese peasants supported the Viet Cong during the Vietnam War. The VC promoted communism, whereas the United States and the government of South Vietnam offered if not democracy, at least a form of government that was not communist. Le Ly Hayslip explains why so many Vietnamese supported the VC and North Vietnamese Army.

Hayslip was a VC cadre member for three years, from the time she was twelve years old. She asserts that the only logical choice for Vietnamese peasants was to support the Viet Cong. The VC taught them that Vietnam was a sovereign nation that should be allowed to govern itself. Hayslip and her villagers were told that Vietnam was divided into two countries simply so the United States could preserve its influence over the country. After the country's freedom and independence had been achieved, the Vietnamese were assured that they would be able to pursue their own dreams of happiness, which to them meant plenty of food and no more war.

Hayslip's devotion to the Viet Cong faded after she had several bad experiences at their hands, including rape, imprisonment, torture, and a death sentence. She ended up marrying an American. She and her husband went to the United States in 1972. Charles Jay Wurts is the coauthor of *When Heaven and Earth Changed Places,* from which this selection is taken.

For my first twelve years of life, I was a peasant girl in Ky La, now called Xa Hoa Qui, a small village near

Excerpted from *When Heaven and Earth Changed Places*, by Le Ly Hayslip, with Charles Jay Wurts. Copyright © 1989 by Le Ly Hayslip and Charles Jay Wurts. Reprinted by permission of Doubleday, a division of Random House, Inc.

Danang in Central Vietnam. My father taught me to love god, my family, our traditions, and the people we could not see: our ancestors. He taught me that to sacrifice one's self for freedom—like our ancient kings who fought bravely against invaders; or in the manner of our women warriors, including Miss Trung Nhi Trung Trac who drowned herself rather than give in to foreign conquerors—was a very high honor. From my love of my ancestors and my native soil, he said, I must never retreat.

From my mother I learned humility and the strength of virtue. I learned it was no disgrace to work like an animal on our farm, provided I did not complain. "Would you be less than our ox," she asked, "who works to feed us without grumbling?" She also taught me, when I began to notice village boys, that there is no love beyond faithful love, and that in my love for my future husband, my ancestors, and my native soil, I must always remain steadfast.

For my next three years of life, I loved, labored, and fought steadfastly for the Viet Cong against American and South Vietnamese soldiers.

Everything I knew about the war I learned as a teenaged girl from the North Vietnamese cadre leaders in the swamps outside Ky La. During these midnight meetings, we peasants assumed everything we heard was true because what the Viet Cong said matched, in one way or another, the beliefs we already had.

## The Lessons Learned

The first lesson we learned about the new "American" war was why the Viet Cong was formed and why we should support it. Because this lesson came on the heels of our war with the French (which began in 1946 and lasted, on and off, for eight years), what the cadre leaders told us seemed to be self-evident.

First, we were taught that Vietnam was *con rong chau tien*—a sovereign nation which had been held in thrall by Western imperialists for over a century. That all nations had a right to determine their own destiny also seemed beyond dispute, since we farmers subsisted by our own hands and felt we owed nothing to anyone but god and our ancestors for the right to live as we saw fit. Even the Chinese, who had made their own disastrous attempt to rule Vietnam in centuries past, had learned a painful lesson about our country's zeal for independence. "Vietnam," went the saying that summarized their experience, "is nobody's lapdog."

Second, the cadres told us that the division of Vietnam into North and South in 1954 was nothing more than a ploy by the defeated French and their Western allies, mainly the United States, to preserve what influence they could in our country.

"*Chia doi dat nuoc?*" the Viet Cong asked, "Why should outsiders divide the land and tell some people to go north and others south? If Vietnam were truly for the Vietnamese, wouldn't we choose for ourselves what kind of government our people wanted? A nation cannot have *two* governments," they said, "anymore than a family can have two fathers."

Because those who favored America quickly occupied the seats of power formerly held by the French, and because the North remained pretty much on its own, the choice of which side best represented independence was, for us, a foregone conclusion. In fact, the Viet Cong usually ended our indoctrination sessions with a song that played on our worst fears:

> Americans come to kill our people,
> Follow America, and kill your relatives!
> The smart bird flies before it's caught.
> The smart person comes home before Tet.
> Follow us, and you'll always have a family.
> Follow America, and you'll always be alone!

## A Choice Between Two Leaders

After these initial "lessons," the cadre leaders introduced us to the two Vietnamese leaders who personified each view— the opposite poles of our tiny world. On the South pole was President Ngo Dinh Diem, America's staunch ally, who was Catholic like the French. Although he was idolized by many who said he was a great humanitarian and patriot, his religion alone was enough to make him suspicious to Buddhists on the Central Coast. The loyalty we showed him, consequently, was more duty to a landlord than love for a founding father. Here is a song the Republican schoolteachers made us learn to praise the Southern president:

> In stormy seas, Vietnam's boat rolls and pitches.
> Still we must row; our President's hand upon the helm.
> The ship of state plows through heavy seas,
> Holding fast its course to democracy.
> Our President is celebrated from Europe to Asia,
> He is the image of philanthropy and love.
> He has sacrificed himself for our happiness.
> He fights for liberty in the land of the Viet.
> Everyone loves him earnestly, and behind him we will march
> Down the street of freedom, lined with fresh flowers,
> The flag of liberty crackling above our heads!

## Uncle Ho

In the North, on the other pole, was Ho Chi Minh, whom we were encouraged to call *Bac Ho*—Uncle Ho—the way we would refer to a trusted family friend. We knew nothing of his past beyond stories of his compassion and his love for our troubled country—the independence of which, we were told, he had made the mission of his life.

Given the gulf between these leaders, the choice of whom we should support again seemed obvious. The cadre leaders encouraged our natural prejudices (fear of outsiders and love of our ancestors) with stirring songs and tender stories about Uncle Ho in which the Communist leader and our ancient heroes seemed to inhabit one congenial world. Like an unbroken thread, the path from our ancestors and legends seemed to lead inevitably to the Northern leader—then past him to a future of harmony and peace.

But to achieve that independence, Ho said, we must wage total war. His cadremen cried out "We must hold together and oppose the American empire. There is nothing better than freedom, independence, and happiness!"

# Freedom, Independence, Happiness

To us, these ideas seemed as obvious as everything else we had heard. *Freedom* meant a Vietnam free of colonial domination. *Independence* meant one Vietnamese people—not two countries, North and South—determining its own destiny. *Happiness* meant plenty of food and an end to war— the ability, we assumed, to live our lives in accordance with our ancient ways. We wondered: how can the Southerners oppose these wonderful things? The answer the Viet Cong gave us was that the Republicans prized Yankee dollars more than the blood of their brothers and sisters. We did not think to question with our hearts what our minds told us must be true.

Although most of us thought we knew what the Viet Cong meant by freedom, independence, and happiness, a few of us dared to ask what life the Northerners promised when the war was over. The answer was always the same: "Uncle Ho promises that after our victory, the Communist state will look after your rights and interests. Your highest interest, of course, is the independence of our fatherland and the freedom of our people. Our greatest right is the right to determine our own future as a state." This always brought storms of applause from the villagers because most people remembered what life was like under the French.

# Clinging to a Vision

Nonetheless, despite our vocal support, the Viet Cong never took our loyalty for granted. They rallied and rewarded and lectured us sternly, as the situation demanded, while the Republicans assumed we would be loyal because we lived south of a line some diplomats had drawn on a map. Even when things were at their worst—when the allied forces devastated the countryside and the Viet Cong themselves resorted to terror to make us act the way they wanted—the villagers clung to the vision the Communists had drummed into us. When the Republicans put us in jail, we had the image of "Communist freedom"—freedom from war—to see us through. When the Viet Cong executed a relative, we convinced ourselves that it was necessary to bring "Communist happiness"—peace in the village—a little closer. Because the Viet Cong encouraged us to voice our basic human feelings through patriotic songs, the tortured, self-imposed silence we endured around Republicans only made us hate the government more. Even on those occasions when the Republicans tried to help us, we saw their favors as a trick or sign of weakness. Thus, even as we accepted their kindness, we despised the Republicans for it.

As the war gathered steam in the 1960s, every villager found his or her little world expanded—usually for the worse. The steady parade of troops through Ky La meant new opportunities for us to fall victim to outsiders. Catholic Republicans spurned and mistreated Buddhists for worshiping their ancestors. City boys taunted and cheated the "country bumpkins" while Vietnamese servicemen from other provinces made fun of our funny accents and strange ways. When the tactics on both sides got so rough that people were in danger no matter which side they favored, our sisters fled to the cities where they learned about liquor, drugs, adultery, materialism, and disrespect for their ancestors. More than one village father died inside when a "stranger from Saigon" returned in place of the daughter he had raised.

## Our Neighbors

In contrast to this, the Viet Cong were, for the most part, our neighbors. Even though our cadre leaders had been trained in Hanoi, they had all been born on the Central Coast. They did not insult us for our manners and speech because they had been raised exactly like us. Where the Republicans came into the village overburdened with American equipment designed for a different war, the Viet Cong made do with what they had and seldom wasted their best ammunition—the goodwill of the people. The cadremen pointed out to us that where the Republicans wore medals, the Viet Cong wore rags and never gave up the fight. "Where the Republicans pillage, rape, and plunder," they said, "we preserve your houses, crops, and family"; for they knew that it was only by these resources—our food for rations, our homes for hiding, our sons and brothers for recruits—that they were able to keep the field.

## Imperialist Aggression

Of course, the Viet Cong cadremen, like the Republicans, had no desire (or ability, most of them) to paint a fairer picture. For them, there could be no larger reason for Americans fighting the war than imperialist aggression. Because we peasants knew nothing about the United States, we could not stop to think how absurd it would be for so large and wealthy a nation to covet our poor little country for its rice fields, swamps, and pagodas. Because our only exposure to politics had been through the French colonial government (and before that, the rule of Vietnamese kings), we had no concept of democracy. For us, "Western culture" meant bars, brothels, black markets, and *xa hoi van minh*—bewildering machines—most of them destructive. We couldn't imagine that life in the capitalist world was anything other than a frantic, alien terror. Because, as peasants, we defined "politics" as something other people did someplace else, it had no relevance to our daily lives—except as a source of endless trouble. As a consequence, we overlooked the power that lay in our hands: our power to achieve virtually anything we wanted if only we acted together. The Viet Cong and the North, on the other hand, always recognized and respected this strength.

We children also knew that our ancestral spirits demanded we resist the outsiders. Our parents told us of the misery they had suffered from the invading Japanese ("small death," our neighbors called them) in World War II, and from the French, who returned in 1946. These soldiers destroyed our crops, killed our livestock, burned our houses, raped our women, and tortured or put to death anyone who opposed them—as well as many who did not. Now, the souls of all those people who had been mercilessly killed had come back to haunt Ky La—demanding revenge against the invaders. This we children believed with all our hearts. After all, we had been taught from birth that ghosts were simply people we could not see.

## Called to War

There was only one way to remove this curse. Uncle Ho had urged the poor to take up arms so that everyone might be guaranteed a little land on which to cultivate some rice. Because nearly everyone in Central Vietnam was a farmer, and because farmers must have land, almost everyone went to war: with a rifle or a hoe; with vigilance to give the alarm; with food and shelter for our fighters; or, if one was too little for anything else, with flowers and songs to cheer them up. Everything we knew commanded us to fight. Our ancestors called us to war. Our myths and legends called us to war. Our parents' teachings called us to war. Uncle Ho's cadre called us to war. Even President Diem had called us to fight for the very thing we now believed he was betraying—an independent Vietnam. Should an obedient child be less than an ox and refuse to do her duty?

And so the war began and became an insatiable dragon that roared around Ky La. By the time I turned thirteen, that dragon had swallowed me up.

# Capturing an American Pilot

Van Anh

A soldier in the North Vietnamese Army, Van Anh tells of how the unit he was with in the jungles of Vietnam shot down an American airplane. He and his fellow soldiers captured the pilot and using his uniform and supplies, set a trap to shoot down more Americans who would be coming to search for him the next morning. Despite an unexpected reaction by the rescuers, the Vietnamese were successful in their plan. Van is very proud of how his unit managed to trick the Americans and shoot down the rescue helicopter.

Anh's account appeared in *A Vietcong Memoir* and *Vietnam: A Portrait of Its People at War*, by David Chanoff and Doan Van Toai.

In June 1964 fleets of American jet planes started appearing in the Laotian skies. Often they'd come twice a day, at about nine in the morning and then at three in the afternoon. They seemed like tiny arrows, white against the blue sky. Behind them they left a white line of smoke and a jet sound that excited the curiosity of people like us who had lived for a long time in the jungle and had never seen any jets before.

Word was passed around that these jets didn't actually bomb, they only observed. We believed that, and many of us were less than prudent. Sometimes we came out of our huts in white shirts to watch them fly by. It was exciting to watch

Excerpted from *"Vietnam": A Portrait of Its People at War*, by David Chanoff and Doan Van Toai (New York: I.B. Tauris, 1996). Copyright © 1986 by David Chanoff and Doan Van Toai. Reprinted by permission of the publisher.

and safe enough. But if the older T-28s came close we hid. We were located on a mountain, and we cleared an area for an observation post high enough to observe the planes when they appeared. At that time our unit had no antiaircraft guns. With our ordinary weapons, we could hit a plane only if it flew nearby and low to the ground.

One day, at noon, we heard the sound of antiaircraft fire from Xieng Khoang, a nearby town. The sound alarmed us, and we positioned all the guns in that direction. This time we didn't just watch. Suddenly an F-101 jet appeared, very low. We didn't even hear its sound before it was on us. We were all shooting, without stop. Then the plane was on fire and we saw something come out of it. Somebody said, "Look, two parachutes!" But we saw only one pilot; the other thing seemed to be his chair.

The pilot came down into the jungle about three kilometers [two miles] away. We ran, struggling against time to get to the place where he fell before his comrades could get to him. About fifteen minutes after he parachuted, the sky was full of jets, helicopters, and an L-19 spotter plane. We climbed the mountain, past the waterfall while they circled around, looking for him in the wrong place. It took us almost six hours to find and capture him, but by then the sky had clouded over, and the planes couldn't see anything underneath.

At six-thirty in the evening, we listened to BBC radio reporting the loss of the jet and that bad weather had prevented rescuers from finding the pilot. It said that rescue efforts would begin again the next morning. At 9 p.m. Voice of America broadcast the same news. None of them knew that the pilot was in our hands.

The pilot's belongings consisted of a small flare gun to signal searchers, a flashlight that gave off a very strong line of light that could signal in the dark, and a life jacket that could filter seawater into drinking water. We knew that this pilot might be someone important and dangerous. The battalion commander told another comrade and me to write down the interrogation. This was the first time in my life I had met an American. When I entered the room, the pilot was struggling with fleas, moving around close to the fire to try to get them off. Here in the mountains of Laos, the popular song said, "Yellow flies, fleas and wind in Pha-Ka are most dangerous and impossible to stop." The only way to keep these flies and fleas off was to heat your clothes up. Then they would jump off. The fleas would always attack strangers. We used to burn jungle leaves to keep them off, but it didn't help much.

None of us could speak English well, so sometimes it was as if he were mute and we were deaf. We wrote down only what we needed to know, in our broken English. Our purpose in this urgent interrogation was to know the code words he would use to contact his friends when they tried to save him. Dr. Ngoc was the only one who acted as an interrogator.

After we got everything we needed for that moment, I went into the staff headquarters cottage to discuss plans. The atmosphere was serious. No one was in favor of moving out to escape the American search teams that would be coming the next day. We all wanted to wait to take some counteraction against them. We discussed over and over a plan and all the details. Then we called in all the company commanders to give them their orders.

Outside the cottage the soldiers were excited about this capture. They were all awake, talking about the first American they had ever met, and they were all happy about the victory.

## A Plan to Attack the Rescuers

According to the plan, Comrade Hoang De, the battalion chief of staff, would play the role of the American pilot. Hoang De was tall and fat, maybe the largest person in the whole force; he would wear the pilot's clothes and use the code signals to attract the teams that would come searching. He would lie down in an area of the Doi Tron Mountain that would be most advantageous for us. I would be closest to him, to give him support or to rescue him if it was necessary. Two B-40s [hand-held rocket launchers) were positioned to cover the area. Other big guns and automatic weapons were also zeroed in.

The next morning at about seven a spotter plane appeared, then two groups of T-28s flew in and rocketed around the mountain. Thirty minutes later, two units of jets came in to rocket and bomb. Now we realized that the jets could certainly attack, not just observe, and they could attack a lot more powerfully than the T-28s. Finally, two helicopters appeared. I hid myself in the brush and gripped my AK.

Hoang De was wearing the black pilot's uniform and his red hat with a visor. The hat partially covered his eyes and face, so that they wouldn't recognize that he was Vietnamese. He ran into an area where the spotter plane could get a clearer view of him, about a hundred and fifty meters away from me. Then Hoang De shot the flare gun to signal them, first one shot, then two more.

## The Rescue Attempt

The spotter plane saw it and immediately flew in toward Hoang De to get a closer look. From where I was I could see the pilot very clearly. I was afraid he would see that Hoang De wasn't the right person. Then the helicopter lowered down, looking like a dragonfly. Hoang De half-walked, half-crawled, as if he were wounded. It was partly an act, but partly it was because he was wearing the pilot's shoes. Now he was only about fifty meters away from me. I kept thinking about his shoes, that if something happened he wouldn't be able to move quickly.

The helicopter hovered there, lower, lower, about thirty meters from the ground. The jets circled around to give support. Now Hoang De was in a totally clear area. I could see two Americans in the helicopter with their hands on their guns, ready to shoot. Hoang De stood up slowly and with difficulty. The helicopter lowered a long cable toward him. Then a head emerged from the helicopter—a red face, high nose, and brown hair. The man shouted something at Hoang De. I thought, Oh my God, Hoang De can't speak English. And even if he could, how could he reply without showing that he is Vietnamese?

I was really scared. It was the first time I had faced the

American Air Force—helicopter, jets, spotter plane, everything. We didn't have enough weapons to counter them. I didn't have any idea what to do.

Suddenly Hoang De ran forward a few steps and fell down. The white bandage he had wrapped around his leg was clearly visible, and he lay there as if he were dead. I thought, What a reaction! What a great idea! They wanted him to answer, maybe they suspected something. But there he was, unconscious.

The American with the red face stuck his head out as far as he could to look, then another American stuck his head out. I wondered if they would set the helicopter down or if they would leave. But it still hovered there at the same height, no lower, no higher. They hesitated to make their decision.

Hoang De knew this was the crucial moment. Maybe he thought they had found him out, or that they would get away. Suddenly he shouted, "Fire!" The two B-40s roared. The helicopter was hit and exploded, then fell to the ground. Hoang De and I ran as fast as we could to hide. We were safely inside the bunker when the jets bombed the area. But after a while they left.

## In Retrospect

While the air strikes were hitting around the bunker, I was thinking of the scene. We had had many options. We could have forced Sa [the pilot]to call the rescue team and have them land. But we could have done that only if the pilot had agreed. But there were no guarantees. He might have agreed, then when they came in he could have changed his mind and told them the truth. How could we know? We couldn't stand alongside him to guard against it.

As it was, we didn't expect that the rescue team would try to speak to the pilot to check. But they were smart enough to do that. So Hoang De's quick decision to fall and pretend to be unconscious was a wonderful resolution. And when Hoang De shouted, "Fire!" it was at just the right moment. Who could tell if the rescue team was about to find out that he wasn't the right person?

# Living in the Jungle

Truong Nhu Tang, with David Chanoff and Doan Van Toai

Truong Nhu Tang, a founder of the National Liberation Front, the political wing of the Viet Cong, was Minister of Justice in the VC's Provisional Revolutionary Government. He led a double life in Saigon as a high-level official in the South Vietnamese government while he was a member of the Viet Cong. He was captured and tortured by the South Vietnamese government, but after he was released in 1968 in a secret U.S.-VC prisoner exchange, he spent the rest of the war living in the South Vietnamese jungle near the border of Cambodia. In the following excerpt, he discusses a few of the hardships the VC endured during the war.

Life in the jungle was not easy for the Viet Cong. The soldiers lived like hunted animals, trying to avoid detection by American troops and planes. Their living conditions were primitive; there was no electricity or running water and all drinking water had to be boiled first. They had few personal possessions because they had to be ready to move at any moment. They lived on rice and not much else. Mosquitoes—and the malarial disease they carried—venomous snakes, tigers, leeches, and other animals posed a constant danger to the cadres. Most VC were separated from their families for extended periods of time.

After the war, Truong became disillusioned with the Communist government and escaped by boat to a refugee camp. He now lives in Paris, France. David Chanoff and Doan Van Toai are coauthors of *Vietnam: Portrait of the Enemy* and *A Vietcong Memoir*, from which this selection is excerpted.

Excerpted from *A Vietcong Memoir*, by Truong Nhu Tang, with David Chanoff and Doan Van Toai (New York: Vintage Books, 1987). Copyright © 1986 by Truong Nhu Tang, David Chanoff, and Doan Van Toai. Used by permission of the authors.

It was along the Vam Co River some miles below NLF [National Liberation Front, the political wing of the Viet Cong] headquarters that we chose sites for the various PRG [Provisional Revolutionary Government, established by the NLF] ministries. This rugged and heavily forested area, flanking the Cambodian border and deep within the "Iron Triangle" of sanctuaries and bases, provided as good protection as we could get from the marauding B-52s and helicopter-borne assaults. Here we could have easy communication with COSVN [Central Office, South Vietnam, the Communist headquarters in South Vietnam] on the Mimot plantation to our north and immediate access to the emergency escape routes across the frontier. As work on bunkers and shelters for the Justice Ministry progressed, I began to get accustomed to life in the jungle.

## Life in the Jungle

Before too long the urbanites of the PRG had settled into an existence that contrasted dramatically with their previous life-styles. Except for several interruptions for diplomatic missions, this jungle dweller's life was to be mine for the next six years. With some minor exceptions, it was a life shared by all the guerrillas, from PRG President Huynh Tan Phat down to the lowliest messenger boy. Those of us in the ministries had our supplies carried for us when we were on the move and our food cooked, but these perquisites did little to affect the sense of close fellowship that touched almost everyone.

If anything set the leadership apart, it was our access to information. Aside, of course, from the daily briefings, we had the Saigon newspapers and our personal radios, on which we could tune in to the BBC or Voice of America as well as to the Vietnamese stations (North and South) and the Australian Vietnamese language broadcasts. (Those few fighting men who did have radios were strictly forbidden to monitor enemy stations.) These sturdy, Japanese-made transistors—a hundred of them—had been a gift to Ho Chi Minh from the Japanese Communist Party, symbols perhaps of the relentless spread of Japanese technology. (Later we would acquire large numbers of Honda motorbikes.) Ho apparently couldn't find any better use for them than to give them, as his own gifts, to the PRG and Alliance leadership.

But despite the radios, life's conspicuous features were the same for everyone. We lived like hunted animals, an existence that demanded constant physical and mental alertness. In the Iron Triangle, wariness and tension were the companions of every waking moment, creating stresses that were to take an increasing toll on our equanimity as the American bombers closed in on the bases and sanctuaries in late 1969 and 1970.

Ready to move at any instant, we kept our personal encumbrances to a minimum. Two pairs of black pajamas, a couple of pairs of underpants, a mosquito net, and a few square yards of light nylon (handy as a raincoat or roof) were all that a guerrilla owned. The fighters, of course, carried weapons and ammunition in addition, as well as "elephant's intestines," our term for the long tubes of rolled cotton that could be filled with rice and slung across the back.

## Food

In addition to rice, each man's personal larder was rounded out by a small hunk of salt, a piece of monosodium glutamate, and perhaps a little dried fish or meat. The rice ration for both leaders and fighters was twenty kilos a month. Eaten twice a day, at about nine in the morning and four in the afternoon, the ration did not go far. But by and large it was our entire diet, a nutritional intake that left us all in a state of semistarvation.

Under these circumstances, food was a continual preoccupation; the lack of protein especially drove us to frenzied efforts at farming or hunting whenever it was feasible. Occasionally units would be stationed in one place long enough to raise chickens or even pigs. I will always remember one chicken feast, where we shared out a single bird among almost thirty of us, cutting it into the smallest possible bits and savoring each shred. I think I have never eaten anything quite so delicious.

Rarely, some sort of special shipment would come in from Cambodia, occasioning real celebrations. More often the guerrillas would go off on ad hoc hunting expeditions, returning at times with kills of every description. Elephants, tigers, wild dogs, monkeys—none of these were strangers to our cookpots. Still, even protein-starved as I was, I had a hard time choking down monkey meat or dog. Some people think of dog as a Vietnamese delicacy. But, in fact, it is only native to the Northern cuisine. Southerners tend to regard it with the same sort of distaste Westerners might. Elephant is another unappetizing item, a tasteless rubbery substance as tough as old shoes. Dried, it was slightly more palatable.

Another dietary supplement which I eventually learned to eat—if not with relish, then at least without gagging—was jungle moth. Often, as we sat around our oil lanterns at night, talking or going over plans, we would catch the big moths fluttering around the light. With the wings off and barbecued quickly over a flame, it wasn't exactly a tasty morsel, but it wasn't that bad either. All this was a far cry from the carefully prepared dining my mandarin upbringing had taught me to enjoy, a contrast that provided a bit of sardonic merriment for those of us who had traded in Saigon's comforts for the uncertain hospitality of the jungle. Sometime during the second or third year after my release from prison, most of the exotic fare no longer appeared on our jungle menu. By then the tigers, elephants, and monkeys had all but vanished from the forest—into the stomachs of the guerrillas.

## Purchasing Supplies

In addition to our clothing and rations, each of us received pay of either sixty or seventy-five piasters a month—the leadership cadres getting the extra fifteen. (Sixty piasters at that time equaled about two dollars.) With it we could buy sugar, tobacco, salt, soap, toothbrushes, or some other domestic item by placing an order with the unit's supply cadre. This much-courted individual would travel each month along with the finance cadre to NLF headquarters to pick up the rice allotment and payroll. Once these were distributed, they would hike to Cambodia for the more esoteric purchases requested by their units. When I first arrived, their habit was simply to go to any of the border-area towns for their marketing. But later, Cambodian businessmen set up special, more convenient trade outlets, a kind of Vietcong jungle PX.

Although the Cambodian markets were favored for the security they afforded, the Vietnamese villages in the vicinity occasionally provided supplies unavailable elsewhere—especially after 1970. Up till then our usual means of transportation was bicycle or foot. But in the winter of 1969–1970 the whole country was inundated by an invasion of Japanese motorbikes. In one way or another, these bikes made

# The Surrender of Saigon

*The United States officially withdrew all its armed forces from Vietnam in March 1973 after several years of peace negotiations. The South Vietnamese were unable to hold out against the North Vietnamese Army and city after city fell to the NVA. On April 30, 1975, with the Communist forces closing in, U.S. Marines helped evacuate from the American embassy in Saigon the few remaining Americans still in Vietnam. Shortly thereafter, Saigon, the capital of South Vietnam, fell to the North Vietnamese.*

*Bui Tin had been a colonel in the North Vietnamese Army but at the time of the surrender he was a journalist working with the NVA. He had been in Saigon in 1973 and so was familiar with the city. He guided the NVA tanks through the streets to the government's palace. Because there was no high-ranking NVA official in the first wave of troops into Saigon, Bui accepted the surrender from General Duong Van Minh, who had been appointed president of South Vietnam earlier that month.*

I didn't really plan on being the one to take the final surrender of the South. It just happened that way. I just hap-

their way out from the cities and into the hands of even the most remote country people, who would then smuggle them to the guerrillas. Quite often the peasants would get their bikes from the local Saigon army forces—in our case the ARVN's [South Vietnamese Army] 5th and 18th Divisions. Eventually, our Finance Department was able to set up regular supply channels directly between these divisions and the Front, forgoing the peasant middlemen.

From that point on we had a regular supply, not just of Hondas, but of typewriters, radios, cigarettes, and a variety of other goods. Before long there was a thriving business between senior officers of these ARVN divisions and the Front in weapons and ammunition as well. Among the most popular items were grenades and Claymore antipersonnel mines. More than a few American soldiers were killed with

---

pened to be with the first tanks to enter the city and so directed them toward the Palace because I knew where it was. None of this was planned. It just happened.

I was directed to General Duong Van Minh by the chief of the guard of the armored unit. I went to General Minh's office. He was standing there, and he said he had been waiting for someone to come in and take the surrender. I looked around and I saw that all of the people in the room were very, very worried. General Minh was dressed in a short-sleeved shirt and his face looked tired. He looked like he had not slept in a long time and he had not shaved for several days. He said he wanted to surrender the government of South Vietnam to me. "I have been waiting since early this morning to transfer power to you," he said. And, of course, I said the now-famous line, "There is no question of your transferring power. Your power has crumbled. You have nothing in your hands to surrender and so you cannot surrender what you do not possess."

Bui Tin, quoted in *Tears Before the Rain: An Oral History of the Fall of South Vietnam*, Larry Engelmann, 1990.

these mines bought from their ARVN comrades. American walkie-talkies were in high demand too, though our troops were used to the Chinese AK47 rifles and never developed much of a taste for the American M-16.

## Malaria

But neither these supply sources nor the matériel flowing down from the North along the Ho Chi Minh Trail alleviated the chronic malnutrition or the tropical diseases that battened on the weakened men. In the jungle the prime enemy was not the Americans or the *nguy* ("puppets," our term for the Saigon government and its troops) but malaria. Very few escaped, and its recurrent attacks ravaged the guerrillas, who called it their jungle tax. For each of my years in the jungle, I spent approximately two months in the hospital, battling the high fevers and general debility of the disease. What with the protracted nutritional deficiencies and the malaria, almost all the jungle dwellers were marked by a jaundiced and sickly pallor. On more than one infiltrating mission this gave them away. Any knowledgeable and semi-observant person could spot a full-time guerrilla at a glance.

Malaria was such a problem that in 1971 Dr. Pham Ngoc Thach, North Vietnam's minister of health, made a study tour of the guerrilla areas as part of an attempt to devise some preventive measures. It was an indication of our medical inadequacies that Dr. Pham himself fell victim to the disease during this tour and died in the jungle. No statistics were ever kept that I know about, but it is certain that we lost more people to malaria than we did to the enemy.

Snakebite was another plague, although antidotes had become widespread by the time I arrived in the jungle. In the tropical swamps and forests, a wide variety of poisonous snakes flourish, and the guerrillas' minimal footwear (mainly rubber thongs) made them especially vulnerable. The most deadly was the *cham quap,* a small brown krait closely resembling a stick and indistinguishable from dry branches in the undergrowth. Its venom took effect almost instantaneously and had to be counteracted by immediately swallowing one snakebite capsule and macerating another to apply to the wound. For years these creatures and others only slightly less toxic had taken a steady toll of lives, and they continued to be a dangerous and painful hazard.

## A Life of Hiding

When neither sick nor fighting, the guerrillas spent their time building bunkers, raising vegetables, and training, constant training. It was a life of hiding and preparation: hiding from attacks, preparing to meet attacks, or training to carry out their own missions. If there was a half-day break in some movement, either away from or toward an engagement, they would dig trenches and bunkers. Food preparation, both in the headquarters complex and on the move, utilized what we called the "cuisine of General Hoang Cam" after a Vietcong general who had devised a system of smokeless cooking. We would build our fires in trenches or depressions, into the dirt sides of which we would dig a horizontal chimney. Almost all the fire's smoke would go into this chimney and be absorbed by the earth, very little of it emerging from the hole at the far end to mark our positions. Over thirty years and more of jungle warfare, the guerrillas had developed many tricks of this sort to shield them from their enemies—tricks that had by this time become second nature.

Training for the NLF fighters included hefty doses of class time, featuring sessions on current news, political and military issues, and the history of the revolution—all intended to strengthen their determination. As a general rule there was no political indoctrination; Marxist subjects, for example, were never touched on. Instead, instructors would devote their attention to elaborating Uncle Ho's great nationalistic slogans: "Nothing Is More Precious Than Independence and Liberty"; "Unity, Unity, Great Unity! Victory, Victory, Great Victory!" and the others. These would be used as homiletic texts, around which would be woven the themes of patriotism and the sacred duty of expelling the Americans.

Among the Northern troops the curriculum differed considerably. Having grown to manhood in the austere Marxist climate of the DRV [Democratic Republic of Vietnam (North Vietnam)], they were used to taking their ideology straight, and their political cadres and instructors kept up a steady infusion of Marxist precepts and class analysis. Had we attempted similar indoctrination of the Southern peasant guerrillas, they would have considered it worse torture than the regime could possibly devise for them.

## Breaks in the Routine

The harshness of this life amidst the septic jungle, with its continual training and constant watchfulness, was occasionally broken by a visit from an entertainment unit, running movies or staging a show. For the most part, their plays and songs were on standard subjects: guerrilla warfare, revolutionary heroes, ethnic folkways, and the like. But they were always welcomed enthusiastically for the relief they provided from a rigorous and danger-filled routine.

Even more welcome were the leaves of absence that the guerrillas were periodically granted. Those who came from the countryside could make their own arrangements to get back home and visit their families. But for the city dwellers, the logistics were more difficult. Infiltrating into areas under secure government control to see wives and children who had often been marked as Vietcong dependents was a chancy business. To get around this, from time to time we would be able to bring families out to the jungle, something that was done for soldiers as well as cadres. But such meetings were necessarily brief and dangerous themselves. (Vo Van Kiet's wife and children were killed on their way to one such rendezvous, when they were caught in a B-52 raid.) More often than not these men went for extended periods without any contact at all with their families.

## B-52 Attacks

But for all the privations and hardships, nothing the guerrillas had to endure compared with the stark terrorization of the B-52 bombardments. During its involvement, the United

States dropped on Vietnam more than three times the tonnage of explosives that were dropped during all of World War II in military theaters that spanned the world. Much of it came from the high altitude B-52s, bombs of all sizes and types being disgorged by these invisible predators. The statistics convey some sense of the concentrated firepower that was unleashed at America's enemies in both North and South. From the perspective of those enemies, these figures translated into an experience of undiluted psychological terror, into which we were plunged, day in, day out for years on end.

From a kilometer away, the sonic roar of the B-52 explosions tore eardrums, leaving many of the jungle dwellers permanently deaf. From a kilometer, the shock waves knocked their victims senseless. Any hit within a half kilometer would collapse the walls of an unreinforced bunker, burying alive the people cowering inside. Seen up close, the bomb craters were gigantic—thirty feet across and nearly as deep. In the rainy seasons they would fill up with water and often saw service as duck or fishponds, playing their role in the guerrillas' never-ending quest to broaden their diet. But they were treacherous then too. For as the swamps and lowland areas flooded under half a foot of standing water, the craters would become invisible. Not infrequently some surprised guerrilla, wading along what he had taken to be a familiar route, was suddenly swallowed up.

It was something of a miracle that from 1968 through 1970 the attacks, though they caused significant casualties generally, did not kill a single one of the military or civilian leaders in the headquarters complexes. This luck, though, had a lot to do with accurate advance warning of the raids, which allowed us to move out of the way or take refuge in our bunkers before the bombs began to rain down. B-52s flying out of Okinawa and Guam would be picked up by Soviet intelligence trawlers plying the South China Sea. The planes' headings and air speed would be computed and relayed to COSVN headquarters, which would then order NLF or Northern elements in the anticipated target zones to move away perpendicularly to the attack trajectory. Flights originating from the Thai bases were monitored both on radar and visually by our intelligence nets there and the information similarly relayed.

## Total Destruction

Often the warnings would give us time to grab some rice and escape by foot or bike down one of the emergency routes. Hours later we would return to find, as happened on several occasions, that there was nothing left. It was as if an enormous scythe had swept through the jungle, felling the giant teak and go trees like grass in its way, shredding them into billions of scattered splinters. On these occasions—when the B-52s had found their mark—the complex would be utterly destroyed: food, clothes, supplies, documents, everything. It was not just that things were destroyed; in some awesome way they had ceased to exist. You would come back to where your lean-to and bunker had been, your home, and there would simply be nothing there, just an unrecognizable landscape gouged by immense craters.

Equally often, however, we were not so fortunate and had time only to take cover as best we could. The first few times I experienced a B-52 attack it seemed, as I strained to press myself into the bunker floor, that I had been caught in the Apocalypse. The terror was complete. One lost control of bodily functions as the mind screamed incomprehensible orders to get out. On one occasion a Soviet delegation was visiting our ministry when a particularly short-notice warning came through. When it was over, no one had been hurt, but the entire delegation had sustained considerable damage to its dignity—uncontrollable trembling and wet pants the all-too-obvious outward signs of inner convulsions. The visitors could have spared themselves their feelings of embarrassment; each of their hosts was a veteran of the same symptoms.

It was a tribute to the Soviet surveillance techniques that we were caught aboveground so infrequently during the years of the deluge. One of these occasions, though, almost put an end to all our endeavors. Taken by surprise by the sudden earthshaking shocks, I began running along a trench toward my bunker opening when a huge concussion lifted me off the ground and propelled me through the doorway toward which I was heading. Some of my Alliance colleagues were knocked off their feet and rolled around the ground like rag dolls. One old friend, Truong Cao Phuoc, who was working in the foreign relations division, had jumped into a shelter that collapsed on him, somehow leaving him alive with his head protruding from the ground. We extricated him, shoveling the dirt out handful by handful, carefully removing the supporting timbers that were crisscrossed in the earth around him. Truong had been trapped in one of the old U-shaped shelters, which became graves for so many. Later we learned to reinforce these dugouts with an A-frame of timbers that kept the walls from falling in. Reinforced in this manner, they could withstand B-52 bomb blasts as close as a hundred meters.

## Fatalism

Sooner or later, though, the shock of the bombardments wore off, giving way to a sense of abject fatalism. The veterans would no longer scrabble at the bunker floors convulsed with fear. Instead people just resigned themselves— fully prepared to "go and sit in the ancestors' corner." The B-52s somehow put life in order. Many of those who survived the attacks found that afterward they were capable of viewing life from a more serene and philosophical perspective. It was a lesson that remained with me, as it did with many others, and helped me compose myself for death on more than one future occasion.

But even the most philosophical of fatalists were worn to the breaking point after several years of dodging and burrowing away from the rain of high explosives. During the most intense periods we came under attack every day for weeks running. At these times we would cook our rice as soon as we got out of our hammocks, kneading it into glutinous balls and ducking into the bunkers to be ready for what we knew was coming. Occasionally, we would be on the move for days at a time, stopping only to prepare food, eating as we walked. At night we would sling our hammocks between two trees wherever we found ourselves, collapsing into an exhausted but restless sleep, still half-awake to the inevitable explosions.

# The Massacre at My Lai

Ha Thi Qui

The massacre of Vietnamese civilians in My Lai by American troops is a notorious example of the frustration American troops felt fighting a mostly invisible enemy. In the early morning of March 16, 1968, an army platoon led by Lieutenant William L. Calley Jr. entered the hamlet of My Lai (also known as Son My) looking for Viet Cong. The villagers had no reason to fear the soldiers, as American troops had been in the village before. The only people the Americans found in the village were women, children, and old men, but Calley and his troops were taught to suspect everybody of being VC. Accounts of how the massacre began vary, but by the time it ended, between 400 and 600 Vietnamese civilians were dead. The soldiers shot the Vietnamese in their huts and as they stood about in groups in the village. Those who were not killed on the spot were forced to line up next to a ditch where they were shot. Many girls and young women were raped before they were murdered. The Americans then systematically began burning the huts in the village. By late afternoon, My Lai was no more.

Americans did not learn the story of the massacre for two years. Then, twenty-five officers and enlisted men were charged with war crimes, murder, rape, sodomy, and assault on noncombatants. Only Calley was found guilty; he was sentenced to life in prison but was paroled after three years. All the other defendants were acquitted or the charges against them were dismissed.

From "My Lai," by Ha Thi Qui, in *Then the Americans Came: Voices from Vietnam*, by Martha Hess. Copyright © 1993 Martha Hess. Reprinted by permission of the publisher, Four Walls Eight Windows.

> Ha Thi Qui lived in My Lai and managed to survive the massacre by hiding under bodies. Her story of surviving My Lai appears in *Then the Americans Came: Voices from Vietnam*, by Martha Hess.

In the early morning, just after we got up, the helicopters came and started shelling, and soldiers poured out onto the fields. I was eating breakfast. We thought it might be like the other times the Americans came into the village. They gave the children candy. Or like the second time, when Americans came to take water from the well to fill their canteens, and then left, and they didn't do any harm to the people. But the third time, March 16, 1968, when they came to the hamlet they rounded up all the people. Some they took to the roadside and shot right away. The people on the guard tower were all killed. And some they brought over to this ditch, here. First they shot Mr. Cau. He was a monk. He lived in the pagoda. Then they forced everyone into the ditch and shot them. I was wounded in the backside. At first I felt very, very hot, and later on very cold. And they killed—you see, they fired a first time into the ditch, and many men, children and women were killed. They cried, "Mother." They were screaming. The soldiers fired three more times and finished the cries of the people. The first time there were still people screaming. They fired a second time, and the third time it was finished, all the people were killed.

## No Mercy

Afterwards, I got up to go back to my house, and I saw nothing. All the houses had been burned. They had cut down our village tree by the pond. They had cut all the trees down in the orchards. They had killed everyone. There were dead bodies all over the village. I took a little dead baby back to the house from the roadside. It was my daughter's child.

I went to the next hamlet and found my younger sister-in-law killed, lying on the floor. And I found her daughter's body, a fifteen-year-old girl, all her clothing torn off and her legs were spread open—raped by Americans.

They had no mercy, the Americans. You see, they had come here many times and we got along with them. Then they came and killed all the people. They showed no mercy for the people. We had done nothing to them. If they had killed people at the beginning, one or two, we would have known to run, but we didn't know.

I went back to my house and there was nothing, not even a pair of trousers to wear, because everything had been burned. The houses kept on burning, and I couldn't find anyone. I went to another hamlet, untouched by the Americans, to get food and clothing, and told them what had happened at Son My, and they came and carried the dead people away. There was a terrible smell.

My oldest daughter was killed. You bear a child and bring her up, and then she gets killed. My husband had gone to work in the fields very early, so he escaped. Twice before, the Americans had come here and done nothing. We don't understand why the third time they killed the people.

After 1968 we were rounded up and moved to a camp about three, four kilometers from here. The Americans surrounded the camp and we lived inside.

The Americans had lived alongside the Vietnamese people, and we did nothing to them. We worked, spent all our lives in the fields. How could they come and kill us that way? So we are very sad about the massacre, full of sorrow, the village people and the farmers, very sad about it.

# Chronology

**1930**

Ho Chi Minh organizes the Indochinese Communist Party to oppose French colonial rule.

**1932**

**March 9:** Bao Dai, a puppet leader of the French, proclaims himself emperor of Vietnam.

**1941**

**May:** Ho Chi Minh forms the Viet Minh forces to fight the French and Japanese.

**1945**

**July:** At the Potsdam Conference, Vietnam is divided in two along the seventeenth parallel by a demilitarized zone.

**September 2:** Ho Chi Minh declares Vietnam's independence from the French by establishing the Democratic Republic of Vietnam in Hanoi.

**September 26:** The first American adviser is killed in Vietnam. Lieutenant Colonel A. Peter Dewey, head of the Office of Strategic Security (the precurser to the Central Intelligence Agency), is mistaken for a French officer and shot by Communist Viet Minh soldiers.

**1946**

**December 19:** The Indochina War begins when Ho's Viet Minh forces attack French forces in Hanoi.

**1949**

**July:** Bao Dai proclaims the establishment of the State of Vietnam.

## 1950

**January 14:** Ho Chi Minh declares once again that the only legal government of Vietnam is the Democratic Republic of Vietnam.

**January 18:** China recognizes the Democratic Republic of Vietnam.

**February 7:** The United States recognizes Bao Dai's government.

**June 27:** President Harry S. Truman sends military aid to French forces in Vietnam.

**December 30:** The United States, France, Vietnam, Cambodia, and Laos sign a Mutual Defense Assistance Agreement.

## 1954

**May 7:** The Viet Minh defeat the French at Dien Bien Phu.

**July 20–21:** The French sign a cease-fire agreement. Vietnam is divided along the seventeenth parallel. Ho Chi Minh controls North Vietnam; Bao Dai rules South Vietnam.

## 1955

**February 12:** U.S. military advisers start to train South Vietnamese army officers.

**October 26:** Ngo Dinh Diem defeats Bao Dai in a referendum and declares himself president of South Vietnam.

## 1959

**July 8:** Two Americans are killed during an attack at Bien Hoa. Major Dale Buis and Master Sergeant Chester Ovnard are the first Americans to die in combat in Vietnam.

## 1960

**December 20:** The National Liberation Front (NLF)—the Viet Cong—is formed to overthrow the government in South Vietnam.

# 1961

**May:** President John F. Kennedy announces that the United States may have to send troops to Vietnam.

**December 8:** A "white paper" published by the U.S. State Department claims that South Vietnam is threatened by Communist aggression from North Vietnam.

# 1962

**December 31:** The number of military advisers in Vietnam reaches 11,300.

# 1963

**May 1:** Buddhists gather in Hue to protest against the Diem government. Riots ensue for several months.

**June 16:** The first Buddhist monk immolates himself in Saigon.

**August 24:** The U.S. embassy in Saigon receives a cable from Washington that recommends removing Diem from office.

**November 1:** A military coup overthrows President Diem, who is later executed. Diem is replaced by Vice President Nguyen Ngoc Tho and General Duong Van Minh.

# 1964

**January 30:** General Minh is overthrown in another military coup.

**August 2:** The U.S. destroyer *Maddux* is attacked by Vietnamese torpedo boats in the Gulf of Tonkin. A second attack occurs August 4.

**August 5:** Everett Alvarez Jr. is shot down near the North Vietnamese coast and becomes the first American prisoner of war in Vietnam.

**August 7:** Congress approves the Gulf of Tonkin Resolution, which gives President Lyndon B. Johnson the authority to use "all necessary steps, including the use of armed force," to protect any member of the Southeast Asia Treaty

Organization (the United States, France, Britain, Australia, New Zealand, Pakistan, Thailand, and the Philippines).

## 1965

**March 8:** The first American combat troops—3,500 Marines—land at Da Nang.

**April 17:** The Students for a Democratic Society hold the first major antiwar rally in Washington, D.C.

**December 31:** U.S. military personnel in Vietnam officially number 184,300; 636 are listed as killed in action.

## 1966

**April 12:** American B-52s bomb North Vietnam for the first time in retaliation for a Viet Cong attack on U.S. troops.

**July 6:** American POWs are marched through the streets of Hanoi and attacked by an angry mob.

**December 31:** The official number of U.S. military personnel in Vietnam reaches 385,300; 6,644 were killed in action.

## 1967

**September:** General Nguyen Van Thieu is elected president of South Vietnam.

**December 31:** The number of American military personnel in Vietnam is now 485,000; 16,021 are listed as killed in action.

## 1968

**January 21:** The siege of Khe Sanh by the North Vietnamese begins.

**January 31:** The North Vietnamese begin the Tet Offensive, a massive surprise attack against South Vietnam.

**March 16:** Lieutenant William L. Calley and men in his platoon massacre between 400 and 600 Vietnamese civilians in the small village of My Lai.

**March 31:** President Johnson announces he will not run for reelection.

**May 10:** Peace talks between U.S. and Vietnamese officials begin in Paris.

**June 5:** Democratic presidential candidate Robert Kennedy is shot after winning the California primary. He dies the next day.

**October 31:** President Johnson halts the bombing of North Vietnam.

**December 31:** U.S. military personnel in Vietnam officially number 536,600; the number killed in action is 30,610.

## 1969

**March 18:** President Richard M. Nixon approves the secret bombing of Viet Cong bases in Cambodia. The bombings continue through April 1970.

**March 29:** The deaths of 312 U.S. troops during the week of March 23–29 tops the death toll of American fatalities during the Korean War (33,629 fatalities from 1950 to 1953).

**June:** U.S. troop strength peaks at 543,400. President Nixon announces that 25,000 U.S. troops will be withdrawn from Vietnam, the beginning of "Vietnamization."

**September 3:** Ho Chi Minh dies.

**December 31:** The number of U.S. troops in Vietnam declines to 475,000. The number of Americans killed in combat is now 40,024.

## 1970

**February 20:** Henry Kissinger, President Nixon's adviser on national security, meets secretly with North Vietnamese officials in Paris to negotiate a peace treaty.

**April 30:** The U.S. and South Vietnamese armies invade Cambodia to attack North Vietnamese and Viet Cong bases.

**May 4:** Four students are shot and killed by National Guardsmen during an antiwar protest at Kent State University in Ohio.

**June 24:** The U.S. Senate repeals the Gulf of Tonkin Resolution.

**November 21:** American forces raid the prisoner of war camp at Son Tay Prison in North Vietnam. The raid is unsuccessful, however, as the prisoners had been moved several months earlier.

**December 31:** U.S. forces in Vietnam fall to 334,600; 44,245 are listed as killed in action.

## 1971

**February:** South Vietnamese troops, in a test of Vietnamization policy, invade Cambodia. They are decisively beaten.

**March 29:** Lieutenant Calley is the only U.S. service member convicted of the My Lai massacre.

**June 13:** The *New York Times* begins publishing excerpts from the Pentagon Papers, a massive study by the Pentagon on the military policy in Vietnam.

**October 3:** President Thieu is unopposed and reelected as president of South Vietnam.

**December 31:** Almost 200,000 troops have been withdrawn from Vietnam. The official figures of U.S. troops still in Vietnam fall to 156,800; the number of those killed in action is 45,626.

## 1972

**March 30:** The North Vietnamese launch a massive attack on three fronts in South Vietnam called the Spring Offensive.

**April:** U.S. troops left in Vietnam number 69,000.

**May 8:** U.S. forces begin mining Haiphong and other ports in North Vietnam.

**October 21:** The United States and North Vietnam reach a cease-fire agreement.

**December 18:** The "Christmas Bombing Raids" on Hanoi and North Vietnam begin; they go on for eleven days.

**December 31:** U.S. forces in Vietnam number 24,000; the number killed in action rises to 45,926.

## 1973

**January 27:** The United States, South Vietnam, and North Vietnam sign the Paris Peace Accords, ending the U.S. war in Vietnam.

**February–March:** North Vietnam returns 591 American prisoners of war.

**March 29:** The last remaining U.S. combat troops leave Vietnam.

**August 14:** American military operations in Vietnam end.

**December 31:** Only 50 U.S. troops are left in Vietnam. The number of those killed in action is 46,163; it will eventually rise to more than 58,000.

## 1974

**January 4:** The war in South Vietnam resumes.

## 1975

**Spring:** The North Vietnamese Army launches its final offensive against South Vietnam.

**April 21:** President Thieu resigns.

**April 30:** The North Vietnamese Army enters Saigon, the capital of South Vietnam. The remaining Americans and some South Vietnamese in Saigon are evacuated by helicopter from the embassy's roof. The war in Vietnam ends.

## 1977

**January 21:** President Jimmy Carter pardons most Vietnam War draft dodgers.

# For Further Research

Everett Alvarez Jr. and Anthony S. Pitch, *Chained Eagle*. New York: Donald I. Fine, 1989.

Mark Baker, ed., *Nam: The Vietnam War in the Words of the Men and Women Who Fought There*. New York: William Morrow, 1981.

Vaughn Davis Bornet, *The Presidency of Lyndon B. Johnson*. Lawrence: University Press of Kansas, 1988.

Ernest C. Brace, *A Code to Keep: The True Story of America's Longest-Held Civilian Prisoner of War in Vietnam*. New York: St. Martin's Press, 1988.

Matthew Brennan, ed., *Headhunters: Stories from the 1st Squadron, 9th Cavalry in Vietnam, 1965–1971*. Novato, CA: Presidio, 1987.

Philip Caputo, *A Rumor of War*. New York: Ballantine, 1990.

Tom Carhart, *The Offering*. New York: William Morrow, 1987.

David Chanoff and Doan Van Toai, *Vietnam: A Portrait of Its People at War*. New York: I.B. Tauris, 1996.

Philip D. Chinnery, *Life on the Line: Stories of Vietnam Air Combat*. New York: St. Martin's Press, 1988.

Gerald Coffee, *Beyond Survival: A POW's Inspiring Lessons in Living*. New York: Berkley Books, 1991.

Bernard Edelan, ed., *Dear America: Letters Home from Vietnam*. New York: Norton, 1985.

Larry Engelmann, ed., *Tears Before the Rain: An Oral History of the Fall of South Vietnam*. New York: Oxford University Press, 1990.

Daniel E. Evans Jr. and Charles W. Sasser, *Doc: Platoon Medic*. New York: Pocket Books, 1998.

Bill Fawcett, ed., *Hunters and Shooters: An Oral History of the U.S. Navy Seals in Vietnam*. New York: William Morrow, 1995.

Dan Freedman and Jacqueline Rhoads, eds., *Nurses in Vietnam: The Forgotten Veterans*. Austin: Texas Monthly Press, 1987.

Marvin E. Gettleman et al., eds., *Vietnam and America: A Documented History*. Rev. and enlarged 2nd ed. New York: Grove Press, 1995.

Gerald R. Gioglio, ed., *Days of Decision: An Oral History of Conscientious Objectors in the Military During the Vietnam War*. Trenton, NJ: Broken Rifle Press, 1989.

Stanley Goff and Robert Sanders, with Clark Smith, *Brothers: Black Soldiers in the Nam*. New York: Berkley Books, 1985.

Sherry Gershon Gottlieb, *Hell No, We Won't Go! Resisting the Draft During the Vietnam War*. New York: Viking, 1991.

Martha Hess, *Then the Americans Came: Voices from Vietnam*. New York: Four Walls Eight Windows, 1993.

Stanley Karnow, *Vietnam: A History*. Rev. and updated ed. New York: Penguin, 1997.

William R. Kimball, *The Other Side of Glory—Vietnam*. Canton, OH: Daring Books, 1987.

Ron Kovic, *Born on the Fourth of July*. New York: Pocket Books, 1977.

Peter Macdonald, *Giap: The Victor in Vietnam*. New York: Norton, 1993.

Kathryn Marshall, ed., *In the Combat Zone: An Oral History of American Women in Vietnam*. Boston: Little, Brown, 1987.

John McCain with Mark Salter, *Faith of My Fathers*. New York: Random House, 1999.

Tim O'Brien, *If I Die in a Combat Zone: Box Me Up and Ship Me Home*. New York: Laurel, 1987.

Laura Palmer, ed., *Shrapnel in the Heart: Letters and Remembrances from the Vietnam Veterans Memorial.* New York: Random House, 1987.

Lewis B. Puller Jr., *Fortunate Son: The Autobiography of Lewis B. Puller Jr.* New York: Grove Weidenfeld, 1991.

Ben and Anne Purcell, *Love and Duty.* New York: St. Martin's Press, 1992.

Al Santoli, ed., *Everything We Had: An Oral History of the Vietnam War by Thirty-Three American Soldiers Who Fought It.* New York: Ballantine, 1993.

——, ed., *To Bear Any Burden: The Vietnam War and Its Aftermath in the Words of Americans and Southeast Asians.* New York: Dutton, 1985.

Robert D. Schulzinger, *A Time for War: The United States and Vietnam 1941–1975.* New York: Oxford University Press, 1997.

Grace Sevy, ed., *The American Experience in Vietnam: A Reader.* Norman: University of Oklahoma Press, 1989.

Winnie Smith, *American Daughter Gone to War: On the Front Lines with an Army Nurse in Vietnam.* New York: William Morrow, 1992.

Theodore C. Sorensen, ed., *"Let the Word Go Forth": The Speeches, Statements, and Writings of John F. Kennedy, 1947 to 1963.* New York: Laurel, 1991.

Jim and Sybil Stockdale, *In Love and War: The Story of a Family's Ordeal and Sacrifice During the Vietnam Years.* Rev. and updated ed. Annapolis, MD: Naval Institute Press, 1990.

Harry G. Summers Jr., *Vietnam War Almanac.* New York: Facts On File, 1985.

Truong Nhu Tang with David Chanoff and Doan Van Toai, *A Vietcong Memoir.* New York: Vintage Books, 1986.

Wallace Terry, ed., *Bloods: An Oral History of the Vietnam War by Black Veterans.* New York: Random House, 1984.

Lynda Van Devanter with Christopher Morgan, *Home Before Morning: The Story of an Army Nurse in Vietnam.* New York: Warner Books, 1984.

Keith Walker, ed., *A Piece of My Heart: The Stories of Twenty-Six American Women Who Served in Vietnam.* Novato, CA: Presidio, 1997.

William C. Westmoreland, *A Soldier Reports.* Garden City, NY: Doubleday, 1976.

Sanford Wexler, *The Vietnam War: An Eyewitness History.* New York: Facts On File, 1992.

William Appleman Williams et al., eds., *America in Vietnam: A Documentary History.* New York: Norton, 1989.

# Index